This Book Is a Companion Study Guide to the Online Course:

The course is free to all InterNACHI® members.

Upon successfully completing the online course and passing the final exam, you will receive a Certificate of Completion and be able to:

- follow the Standards of Practice for performing an inspection of fireplaces, stoves and chimneys;

- understand how each system and component functions; and

- inspect for and report upon defects observed.

Take the online course at www.nachi.org/inspect-fireplace-stove-chimney-course

How to Inspect Fireplaces, Stoves and Chimneys

The purpose of this publication is to teach inspectors how to inspect fireplaces, wood stoves, and chimneys. This text is designed to augment the student's knowledge in preparation for InterNACHI's online How to Inspect Fireplaces, Stoves, and Chimneys Course and Exam at **www.nachi.org/inspect-fireplace-stove-chimney-course**

To order additional training books, visit www.InspectorOutlet.com

Authors:
Ben Gromicko, Director of Education, International Association of Certified Home Inspectors
Nick Gromicko, Founder, International Association of Certified Home Inspectors, and Founder, International Association of Certified Indoor Air Consultants

Contributors:
Charles Wallace, Chuck Evans, Frank Rotte, Ken Ellison, Nate Snook, Richard Ingalls & Robert Jude

Staff Assistance:
Kim Stover

Graphics:
Levi Nelson, Erica Saurey & Chris Krowiak

Editor:
Kate Tarasenko / Crimea River, LLC

Layout & Design:
Jessica Langer

Copyright © 2021 International Association of Certified Home Inspectors, Inc.

All rights reserved.

The content of this publication, or any part thereof, may not be reproduced in any manner whatsoever without permission in writing from the authors.

www.NACHI.org

Table of Contents

Introduction 5
    Quiz #1 6

Chimney 7
    Chimney and Vent Connection 7
    Inlet 8
    3-2-10 Rule for Masonry Chimneys 8
    Clearance 9
    Masonry Chimney Footing 9
    Quiz #2 10

Chimney Lining 11
    Clay Lining 11
    Metal Flue Lining 12
    Cast-in-Place Lining 12
    Fuel-Gas Termination 12
    Quiz #3 15

Type B & Type L Vents 17
    Type B Vents 17
    Type L Vents 17
    2-2-10 vs. 3-2-10 18
    Quiz #4 19

Corbeling 20
    Chimney Flashing 20
    Chimney Cricket 20
    Chimney Cap (or Crown or Wash) 21
    Quiz #5 22

Fireplace Hearth 23
    Fireplace Lintel 23
    Fireplace Size 23

    Firebox Side and Rear Walls 23
    Fireplace Throat 24
    Fireplace Damper 24
    Fireplace Smoke Shelf 24
    Fireplace Smoke Chamber 24
    Fireplace Ash Dump 25
    Ash Dump Cleanout 25
    Masonry Chimney Cleanout 25
    Exterior Air 26
    Chimney Flue Size 26
    Glass Doors 26
    Quiz #6 27

Factory-Built (Pre-Fabricated) Fireplaces 29
    Factory-Built Chimneys 29
    Panel Walls 30
    Quiz #7 31

Wood-Burning Stoves 32
    Efficiency and Air Pollutants 32
    Quiz 8 34

Initial Inspection 35
    Fireplaces 35
    Hearths, Hearth Extensions and Fire Chambers 35
    Inspection of Single-Wall Metal Chimney 36
    Interior Single-Wall Metal Chimneys 36
    Exterior Single-Wall Metal Chimneys 36
    Chimney Outlets 36
    Flues and Liners 37
    Flue Size 37
    Connectors 40

Cleanouts..40

Preventing Chimney Collapse..................41

Quiz #9..43

Water Damage..44

Water-Damaged Mortar Joints..................44

Install a Cricket to Stop or Prevent Leaks........44

Efflorescence..45

Identifying Efflorescence..........................45

Prevention and Removal of Efflorescence........45

Porous Building Materials..........................46

Capillary Action......................................46

Destructive Pressures..............................46

Spalling..47

Chimney Kickout Flashing..........................47

International Phase I Standards of Practice for Inspecting Fireplaces and Chimneys..............49

Sample Reporting Language......................54

Quiz #10..58

Safe Practices for Fireplaces..............................60

Fireplace Safety for Homeowners...............60

Keep Fireplaces and Wood Stoves Clean........60

Safely Burn Fuels....................................61

Protect the Outside of Your Home...............61

Protect the Inside of Your Home.................61

Fire Extinguishers...................................62

Fire Type..62

Extinguisher Types..................................62

Inspection of Extinguishers.......................63

Extinguisher Testing and Replacement........64

Fireplace Fuel..65

Quiz #11..68

Ventless / Unvented Combustion Appliances....69

Can the health hazards of an unvented heater be reduced?..70

Ventilated Fireplaces................................70

Summary..70

Quiz #12..71

Appendix I: Answer Keys..................................72

Answer Key for Quiz #1............................72

Answer Key for Quiz #2............................72

Answer Key for Quiz #3............................72

Answer Key for Quiz #4............................73

Answer Key for Quiz #5............................74

Answer Key for Quiz #6............................74

Answer Key for Quiz #7............................75

Answer Key for Quiz #8............................75

Answer Key for Quiz #9............................75

Answer Key for Quiz #10..........................76

Answer Key for Quiz #11..........................77

Answer Key for Quiz #12..........................77

Notes..78

Introduction

A visual inspection of the fireplace and chimney is required by InterNACHI's Home Inspection Standards of Practice, which can be read in its entirety at **www.nachi.org/sop**

According to the Standards, the inspector is required to inspect:

- readily accessible and visible portions of all fireplaces and chimneys;
- the lintel above the fireplace opening;
- the damper door by opening and closing it, if readily accessible and manually operable; and
- the cleanout door and frame.

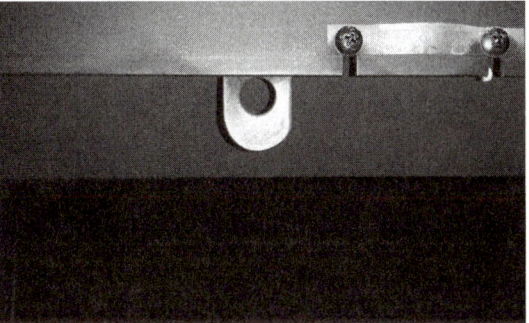

The image at right shows a small handle for operating the manual damper at a pre-fabricated fireplace.

Goal

The goal of the inspection is to provide observations that may lead to the decrease of hazardous conditions associated with fireplaces and chimneys. If the inspection reveals that an existing chimney is not safe for the intended application, it must be repaired, rebuilt, lined, relined, or replaced with a vent or chimney to conform to building standards.

Scope

The scope of the inspection is limited to readily accessible and visible portions of the fireplace and chimney. The inspection is not all-inclusive or technically exhaustive. The inspection involves a visual-only examination the readily accessible portions of the chimney exterior, interior, accessible portions of the appliance, and the chimney connection.

The inspector should look at the general structure of the chimney and any connections to appliances, stoves, and heating systems. The inspector should also look for improper installation, obstructions, and combustible deposits.

The inspector should advise his/her client that all fireplaces, fuel-burning stoves, and chimneys should be inspected by a certified chimney sweep prior to their first use, and not less than annually.

Quiz #1

1. T/F: The inspector is required to inspect the damper doors by opening and closing them, if readily accessible and manually operable.

    ☐ True
    ☐ False

2. The inspection is _____ chimney and fireplace structure, systems and components.

    ☐ an all-inclusive and technically exhaustive evaluation of the
    ☐ a visual-only evaluation of the accessible

3. T/F: The inspector should look at the general structure of the chimney and any connections to appliances, stoves, and heating systems.

    ☐ True
    ☐ False

4. T/F: The inspector should advise his/her client that all fireplaces, fuel-burning stoves, and chimneys should be inspected by a certified chimney sweep prior to their first use, and not less than annually.

    ☐ True
    ☐ False

Answer Key is on page 72.

Chimney

A chimney is a vertical shaft through which smoke and gases from fuel-burning heating systems, stoves, appliances and fireplaces exhaust. The chimney may be built of masonry or metal pipe materials. The flue liner, chimney inner wall, or vent inner wall must be continuous and free of cracks, gaps, perforations, and other damage and deterioration that could allow the escape of combustion products, including gases, moisture and creosote. A solid fuel-burning fireplace, stove, or heating system must not connect to a chimney venting another fireplace, stove, or heating system.

Chimney and Vent Connection

Connectors are used to connect fireplaces, stoves, and heating systems to a vertical chimney or vent, except where the chimney or vent directly is attached.

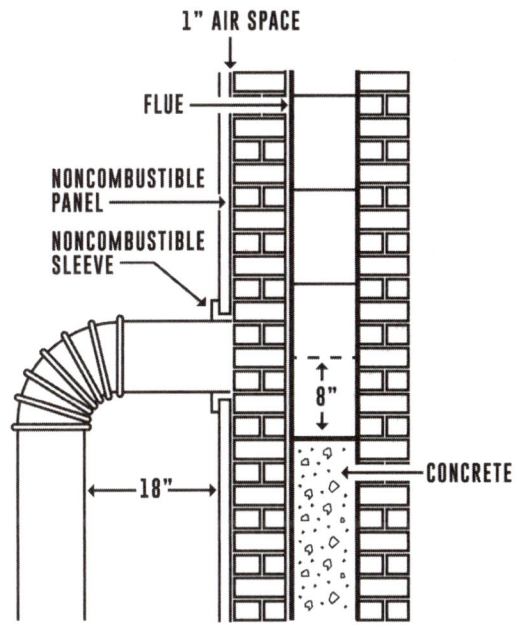

Connectors for oil and solid-fuel burning appliances must be made of factory-built chimney material, Type L vent material, or single-wall metal pipe that is resistant to corrosion and heat. The pipe thickness should be a certain minimum of galvanized steel. For pipes 6 inches or smaller, the minimum is 26-gauge galvanized sheet metal.

Connectors must be accessible or removable for inspection and cleaning. Unused openings in chimneys and vents should be closed.

At a masonry chimney flue, the connector vent pipe must connect at a point at least 12 inches above the lowest portion of the interior of the chimney flue. Some building codes provide for only 8 inches.

Connector vent pipes should be installed in accordance with the manufacturer's installation instructions.

Length and Slope

Stoves and heating systems shall be located as close as is practical to the chimney. Connectors must be as short and as straight as possible. An old general rule of thumb for the maximum length of an uninsulated connector pipe to a natural-draft chimney is 10 feet. The 2018 IRC, Section M1803.3.2, states that the horizontal run of an uninsulated connector pipe to a natural draft chimney should not exceed 75% of the height of the chimney above the connector. The horizontal run of a listed and labeled connector pipe to a natural draft chimney should not exceed 100% of the chimney height above the connector.

Connectors should be sloped at least 1/4-inch of rise per foot of run.

Fastening

Connector joints should be fastened with sheet metal screws or rivets.

Passing Through

A chimney connector pipe or vent connector pipe should not pass through any floor or ceiling. It should not pass through a wall either, unless it's listed and labeled for a wall pass-through.

A single-wall metal pipe used as a vent connector passing through a wall, ceiling or floor must be guarded by a ventilated, non-combustible metal thimble, and must maintain a minimum clearance of 6 inches between the thimble and any combustibles.

A non-combustible thimble must be used where a single-wall metal pipe passes through a roof constructed of combustible material. It would be uncommon to find a single-wall metal pipe passing through a ceiling, wall, floor, or roof. For unlisted single-wall chimneys and vent connectors, a single-wall metal pipe used as a vent connector must maintain a minimum clearance of 18 inches between the metal pipe and any combustibles.

No Reduction

The size of the connector pipe should not be smaller than the flue collar of the appliance. The pipe should not reduce or restrict itself.

Inlet

Inlets to masonry chimneys must enter from the side. Inlets must have a thimble made of fireclay, rigid refractory material, or metal that will prevent the connector from pulling out of the inlet or from extending beyond the wall of the liner.

3-2-10 Rule for Masonry Chimneys

Chimneys should be high enough to prevent downdrafts caused by wind. The 3-2-10 Rule for masonry chimneys states that a masonry chimney should extend at least 3 feet above the highest point where the chimney passes through the roof, and 2 feet above any portion of a building that is within a 10-foot distance horizontally.

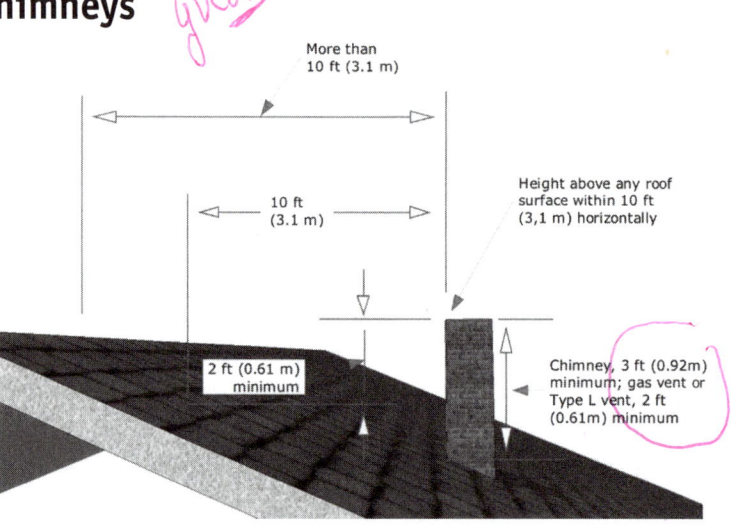

Clearance

House framing components should be at least 2 inches away from the chimney wall. Open spaces between the chimney wall and the combustible building materials should be sealed and insulated with non-combustible material.

Masonry Chimney Footing

A masonry chimney has its own footing and is built in a way such that the chimney provides no support to, nor receives support from, the house structure. The chimney footer may be connected with the house foundation and footing.

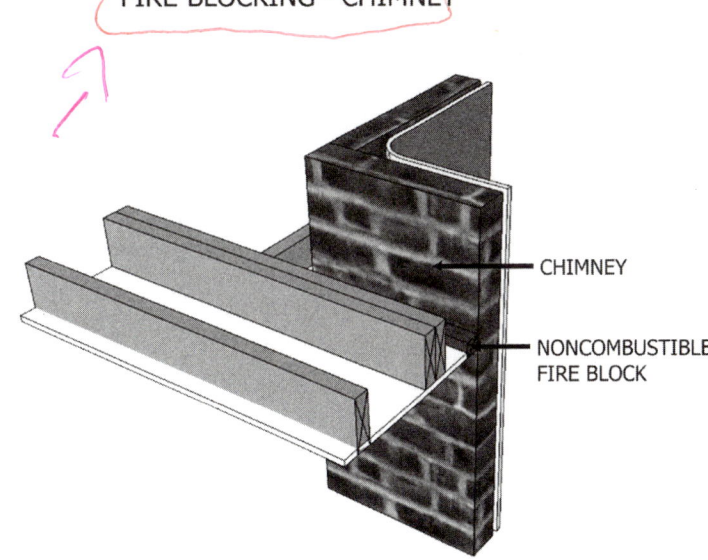

FIRE BLOCKING - CHIMNEY

CHIMNEY

NONCOMBUSTIBLE FIRE BLOCK

Footings for masonry chimneys must be made of concrete or solid masonry at least 1 foot thick. They should extend at least 6 inches beyond the face of the fireplace or foundation wall on all sides. Footings for masonry fireplaces must extend below the frost line. They must be installed on natural, undisturbed earth or engineered fill below frost depth. In climate areas not subject to freezing, the footings should be installed at least 1 foot below the finished grade.

Quiz #2

1. Footings for masonry chimneys must be made of concrete or solid masonry at least _____ thick.

    ☐ 3 feet
    ☐ 1 foot
    ☐ 2 feet

2. The footing for a masonry chimney should extend at least _____ inches beyond the face of the fireplace or foundation wall on all sides.

    ☐ 6
    ☐ 14
    ☐ 24

3. Footings for masonry fireplaces must extend _____ the frost line.

    ☐ below
    ☐ down to
    ☐ above

4. House framing components should be at least ____ inches away from the chimney wall.

    ☐ 6
    ☐ 24
    ☐ 2

5. Open spaces between the chimney wall and the combustible building materials should be sealed and insulated with _____ material.

    ☐ wood shims
    ☐ non-combustible
    ☐ cellulose

6. A masonry chimney should extend at least _____ feet above the highest point where the chimney passes through the roof, and _____ feet above any portion of a building that is within a _____-foot distance horizontally.

    ☐ 3, 10, 2
    ☐ 2, 3, 10
    ☐ 3, 2, 10

7. Inlets to masonry chimneys must enter from the _____.

    ☐ top
    ☐ side
    ☐ bottom

Answer Key is on page 72.

Chimney Lining

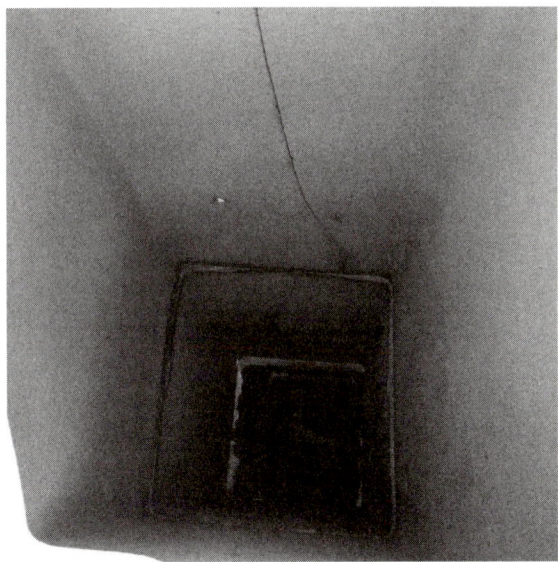

All masonry chimneys must be lined. The chimney lining must be appropriate for the type of fireplace, stove, appliance, or heating system connected to it.

The walls of the masonry chimney having a clay interior flue should be at least 4 inches thick, considering a standard brick is 3-5/8 inches wide. The minimum standard thickness for a flue lining is 5/8-inch thick.

The size of the chimney depends on the number and size of the flues. The flue for a heating system or fireplace should have enough cross-sectional area and height to create an adequate draft.

The image at left shows a deteriorated flue lining, which is a hazard.

Clay Lining

Masonry chimneys can have clay, ceramic, cast-in-place, or metal conduit flue linings. Modern standards require liners to be installed in all masonry chimneys. Unlined chimneys are not safe. A chimney without a flue lining is considered a material defect and should be reported.

The purpose of the flue is to contain the combustion products, direct them to the exterior, and protect the masonry chimney walls from heat and corrosion. A masonry chimney without a flue liner must be professionally inspected and corrected by a certified chimney contractor who will make repairs or replacements so that it meets modern safety standards.

Clay tiles are the most common type of masonry chimney liners. Clay tile flue linings can be square, rectangular or circular. They come in all different sizes, diameters, and cross-sectional pieces. The general rule is that a single flue should be used for only one heating system. You may find the vent from a gas-fired furnace and a gas-fired water tank connected to one flue.

The clay flue lining should extend above the top brick course or masonry cap a minimum of 4 inches. The masonry cap must be sloped in order to direct water away from the flue and off the chimney top. (Refer to the section on chimney caps.)

Metal Flue Lining

Metal chimney flue liners are usually made of stainless steel or aluminum. They are used to upgrade and repair existing masonry chimneys. Stainless steel is suitable for wood-burning, gas, or oil applications. Aluminum is an inexpensive alternative only for certain medium-efficiency gas heating systems.

Cast-in-Place Lining

A cast-in-place chimney flue liner is made of a lightweight, cement-like product installed inside the chimney. The cast-in-place lining is a smooth, seamless stack. It can help correct the structural integrity of an old chimney. Cast-in-place liners are suitable for all fuels.

Fuel-Gas Termination

It is a common mistake to apply the height requirements for chimney terminations (per the 3-2-10 Rule) to fuel vents, which can cause vents to extend above roofs much higher than needed, in most cases. For example, vent pipes terminating above roofs having a slope of up to 6:12 need to be only 1 foot high.

The type of venting materials is dependent upon the operating characteristics of the appliance being vented. Appliances can be characterized with respect to:

- positive or negative pressure within the venting system; and
- whether or not the appliance generates gases that condense in the venting system.

Regardless, all appliances must be connected to venting systems. The venting system must never extend into or pass through any fabricated air duct or furnace plenum. It must convey an adequate, positive flow of flue or vent gases directly to the outdoors.

There are several types of venting systems that can be used, including: plastic piping; special gas vents designed by the manufacturer; and masonry, metal, and factory-built chimneys.

Type of Venting System to Be Used	
Appliance	**Type of Venting System**
• Category I appliances • Appliances with draft hoods • Appliances with Type B vents	• Type B gas vent • Chimney • Single-wall metal pipe • Listed chimney lining for gas venting • Special gas vent listed for the appliance
Listed vent wall furnaces	Type B-W gas vent
Category II appliances	As specified by the manufacturer of the appliance
Category III appliances	As specified by the manufacturer of the appliance
Category IV appliances	As specified by the manufacturer of the appliance
Unlisted appliances	Chimney
Decorative appliances in vented fireplaces	Chimney
Direct-vent appliances	As specified by the manufacturer of the appliance
Appliance with integral vent	As specified by the manufacturer of the appliance

Gas vents that are 12 inches or less in size and located at least 8 feet from a vertical wall or similar structure should terminate above the roof in accordance with the Gas Vent Terminations table to follow.

Gas Vent Terminations	
Roof Pitch	Minimum Height in Feet (& in Meters)
flat to 6/12	1 (0.30)
6/12 to 7/12	1-1/4 (0.38)
over 7/12 to 8/12	1-1/2 (0.46)
over 8/12 to 9/12	2 (0.61)
over 9/12 to 10/12	2-1/2 (0.76)
over 10/12 to 11/12	3-1/4 (0.99)
over 11/12 to 12/12	4 (1.22)
over 12/12 to 14/12	5 (1.52)
over 14/12 to 16/12	6 (1.83)
over 16/12 to 18/12	7 (2.13)
over 18/12 to 20/12	7-1/2 (2.27)
over 20/12 to 21/12	8 (2.244)

These requirements indicate that a greater vent height above the roof is needed as the roof pitch approaches being a vertical surface. The greater the roof slope, the greater the effect of the wind hitting the roof's surface.

Gas vents that are greater than 12 inches in size or that are located less than 8 feet from a vertical wall or similar structure should terminate at least 2 feet above the highest point where they pass through the roof, and not less than 2 feet above any portion of a dwelling within 10 feet horizontally. There are other requirements for direct-vent fireplaces, appliances with integral vents, and appliances using mechanical draft fans.

Quiz #3

1. T/F: Gas vents that are greater than 12 inches in size or that are located less than 8 feet from a vertical wall or similar structure should terminate at least 2 feet above the highest point where they pass through the roof, and not less than 2 feet above any portion of a dwelling within 10 feet horizontally.

    ☐ True
    ☐ False

2. T/F: A greater height for a fuel-gas vent above the roof is needed as the roof pitch approaches being a vertical surface.

    ☐ True
    ☐ False

3. T/F: It is a common mistake to apply height requirements for chimney terminations (such as the 3-2-10 Rule) to fuel vents that cause them to extend above roofs much higher than needed, in most cases.

    ☐ True
    ☐ False

4. T/F: The venting system is permitted to extend into or pass through a fabricated air duct or furnace plenum.

    ☐ True
    ☐ False

5. T/F: A cast-in-place chimney flue liner is made of a lightweight, cement-like product installed inside the chimney.

    ☐ True
    ☐ False

6. A cast-in-place lining _____ help correct the structural integrity of an old chimney.

    ☐ cannot
    ☐ can

7. Metal chimney flue liners are usually made of _____ or aluminum.

    ☐ stainless steel
    ☐ fiberglass
    ☐ cast iron
    ☐ plastic

8. T/F: Stainless steel flue lining is suitable for wood-burning, gas, or oil applications.

- [ ] True
- [ ] False

9. Clay tiles are the _____ common type of masonry chimney liner.

- [ ] most
- [ ] least

10. The general rule is that a single flue should be used for only _____ heating system(s).

- [ ] one
- [ ] three
- [ ] two

Answer Key is on page 72.

Type B & Type L Vents

A Type B or Type L gas vent must terminate at least 5 feet in vertical height above the highest connected appliance's draft hood or flue collar. A Type B-W gas vent must terminate at least 12 feet in vertical height above the bottom of the wall furnace.

Gas vents shall extend through the roof flashing, roof jack, or thimble, and terminate with a listed cap or assembly.

Type B Vents

Type B vents are vents suitable only for listed, draft hood-equipped, gas-fired appliances, including most domestic heating and hot water systems.

They may not be used with any of the following appliances:

- wood-burning appliances, such as fireplaces and wood-burning stoves;
- incinerators;
- oil-fired equipment;
- coal-fired equipment;
- any appliance that burns anything other than liquid petroleum or natural gas; or
- any appliance that produces flue gases that exceed 480° F (249° C);

Type B vents must be equipped with their own special chimney caps. If the cap is damaged or lost, it should not be substituted with something not recommended by the manufacturer. The clearance required from combustible materials is printed on the flue's exterior metal surface, and is generally 1 or 2 inches.

Type L Vents

Type L vents are designed for venting approved oil-fired and natural-gas appliances that produce draft-hood flue gases that do not exceed a temperature of 570° F, or 926° F for 10 minutes in an over-fire situation. The minimum clearance from combustible materials is generally 3 inches. Type L vents should not be used to vent coal- or wood-fired appliances.

It may be difficult to tell the difference between Type L and Type B vents because they are made from similar components, but the vent type should be clearly printed on the vent itself. Both are double-walled, although Type L vents generally have a stainless steel inner wall, while Type B vents do not.

Regardless of the vent type, InterNACHI® inspectors may check for the following defects:

- deterioration of the outer wall, which is likely caused by failure of the inner metal lining;
- violation of roof clearance requirements. All metal vents must terminate at least 2 feet above the roof surface and at least 2 feet above any portion of the building within 10 horizontal feet;

- missing components, such as a chimney cap;

- firestops not installed at either the top or bottom side of the joist where the vent passes through floors or the roof. The firestop should allow a fire-resistance rating equal to or greater than the floor or roof assemblies through which the vent passes;

- blocked bird screens, often caused by freezing moisture in cooler climates;

- crucial joists, rafters or other load-bearing structural members that have been cut to allow for the vent to pass. Plumbing and electrical lines should also not be disturbed by the vent; and

- whether the vent is too high or too low. Manufacturers may set minimum and maximum height requirements for the whole vent assembly, such as the AirJet Type L vent, whose minimum height is 6 feet and maximum height is 30 feet.

Inspectors may recommend that extra corrosion resistance for vents be provided by a stainless steel cap, stainless steel jacketed pipe sections, or stainless steel or aluminum flashings and storm collars. They may also recommend that clients use commercially available combustion-enhancing, acid-neutralizing fuel additives to prevent damage caused to vents by sulfuric acid.

The chimney at left has a loose storm collar. This is a defect.

In summary, Type B and Type L vents are designed to vent gases from specific types of appliances and under certain conditions.

2-2-10 vs. 3-2-10

Type L venting systems should terminate with a listed and labeled cap at least 2 feet above the roof and at least 2 feet above any portion of the building within 10 feet. This is known as the Type L Vent 2-2-10 Rule.

Chimneys should extend at least 2 feet higher than any portion of a building within 10 feet, but shall not be less than 3 feet above the highest point where the chimney passes through the roof. This, again, is known as the Chimney 3-2-10 Rule.

Quiz #4

1. T/F: Chimneys should extend at least 2 feet higher than any portion of a building within 10 feet, but shall not be less than 3 feet above the highest point where the chimney passes through the roof.

    ☐ True
    ☐ False

2. Type L venting systems should terminate with a listed and labeled cap at least _____ feet above the roof and at least _____ feet above any portion of the building within _____ feet.

    ☐ 2, 2, 10
    ☐ 10, 2, 2
    ☐ 3, 2, 10

3. T/F: It may be difficult to tell the difference between Type L and Type B vents because they are made from similar components.

    ☐ True
    ☐ False

4. Type _____ vents are designed for venting approved oil-fired and natural-gas appliances.

    ☐ O
    ☐ L
    ☐ C
    ☐ B

5. T/F: Type L vents must not be used to vent coal- or wood-fired appliances.

    ☐ True
    ☐ False

6. Type _____ vents must be equipped with their own special chimney caps.

    ☐ A
    ☐ L
    ☐ O
    ☐ B

7. Type _____ vents are vents suitable only for listed, draft hood-equipped, gas-fired appliances, including most domestic heating and hot water systems.

    ☐ L
    ☐ A
    ☐ B

Answer Key is on page 73.

Corbeling

Masonry chimneys are sometimes corbeled, which means that several successive courses are extended outward. Sometimes corbeling is observed from the unfinished attic space. Corbeling is usually observed in a location of the chimney just before the chimneystack rises up through the roof.

Masonry chimneys shall not be corbeled more than one-half of the chimney wall's thickness from a wall or foundation. The projection of a single course shall not exceed one-half the unit's height, or one-third of the unit's bed depth, whichever is less.

Chimney Flashing

Chimney flashing should be installed where the chimney stack meets the roof covering to prevent water penetration. Flashing is typically made from corrosion-resistant metal, such as copper. Counter-flashing is installed in the mortar joints and then folded downward to cover the step or base flashing.

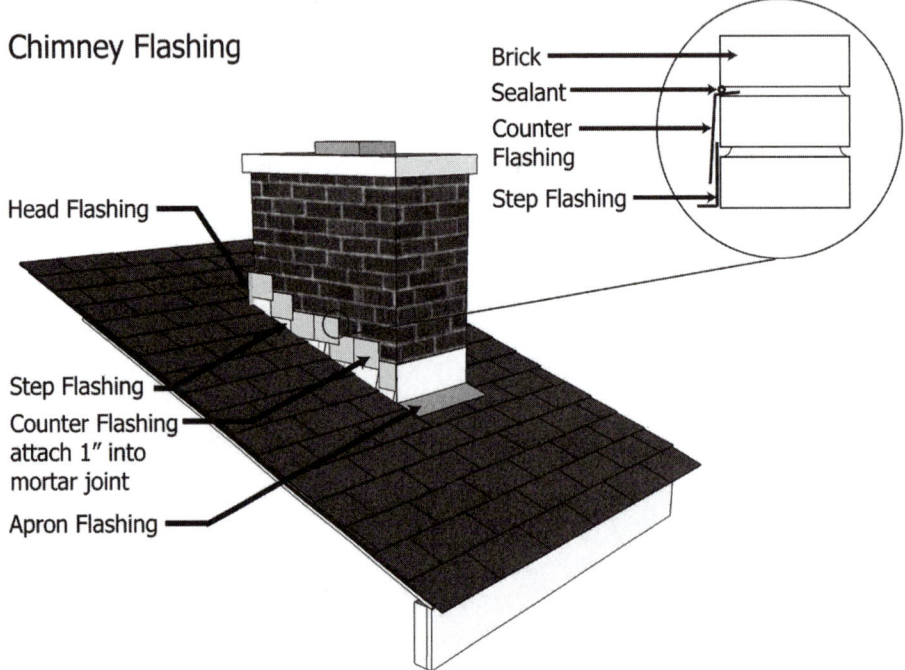

Chimney Cricket

If the chimney has a dimension parallel to the ridgeline greater than 30 inches and does not intersect the ridgeline, a chimney cricket must be provided. Flashing and counter-flashing must be installed at the intersection of the cricket and the chimney. The height of the cricket depends on the slope of the roof. The lower the slope, the shorter the cricket height.

This cricket has heavily applied roof sealant at the valley and ridge. This is a defect.

Chimney Cap (or Crown or Wash)

All masonry chimneys should have a concrete, metal or stone cap. The masonry chimney cap (also referred to as the masonry crown, wash, or splay) is the top element of a masonry chimney. It covers and seals the top of the chimney from the flue liner to the chimney edge. It's often referred to as a crown because of its form and function. Deteriorated masonry was observed at the crown (or wash) pictured at right. This is a defect.

The masonry chimney cap should provide a downward slope that will direct water from the flue to the edge of the cap. The "crowned" cap should be formed so as to shed water.

There should also be a drip edge installed at the cap, as well as a caulked bond break around the flue liner. By directing the runoff from the cap away from the chimney, the overhanging drip edge helps prevent erosion of the brick and mortar in the chimney's vertical surfaces.

Most masonry chimneys are built with an inadequate crown constructed from common mortar mix. The crown must be designed for years of weather abuse without cracking, chipping or deteriorating. A proper chimney crown should be constructed of a Portland cement-based mixture, and cast or formed so it provides an overhang projecting beyond all sides of the chimney by a minimum of 2 inches.

The flue liner tile of a masonry chimney should also project above the crown a minimum of 4 inches.

A metal rain cap and spark arrestor may be installed on a masonry chimney. The chimney pictured above does not have either installed. The arrestor screen should be made of a heat- and corrosion-resistant material, such as galvanized steel (19-gauge) or stainless steel (24-gauge). The screen openings should be sized to allow the passage of a sphere with a diameter between 3/8-inch and 1/2-inch.

The chimney at left has a deteriorated rain cap. This is a defect.

Quiz #5

1. _____ masonry chimneys should have a concrete, metal or stone cap.

    ☐ All
    ☐ Some
    ☐ No

2. The flue liner tile should project above the masonry cap _____.

    ☐ a minimum of 8 inches
    ☐ a minimum of 4 inches
    ☐ at least one-tenth the chimney's height

3. A proper masonry chimney cap should be constructed of a Portland cement-based mixture and cast or formed so it provides an overhang projecting beyond all sides of the chimney by a minimum of _____ inches.

    ☐ 4
    ☐ 2
    ☐ 6

4. Most masonry chimneys are built with an inadequate cap constructed from common _____.

    ☐ mortar mix
    ☐ fiberglass
    ☐ stainless steel

5. The chimney _____ is the top element of a masonry chimney.

    ☐ crown
    ☐ hearth
    ☐ flue

6. If the chimney has a dimension parallel to the ridgeline greater than 30 inches, and does not intersect the ridgeline, a chimney _____ must be provided.

    ☐ kickout flashing
    ☐ brace
    ☐ cricket

7. T/F: Chimney flashing should be installed where the chimney stack meets the roof covering to prevent water penetration.

    ☐ True
    ☐ False

Answer Key is on page 74.

Fireplace Hearth

The hearth is made up of two parts, the front and the back. The front hearth is located in the front of the fireplace combustion chamber, and the back hearth is located within the fireplace combustion chamber. The back hearth is made up of firebrick that can withstand heat from fire.

The hearth is completely supported by the fireplace structure. The hearth is built initially with framing components that make up a temporary support structure. Then concrete is poured and reinforcement is installed in the pour. The temporary support is removed after the concrete is completely cured. No combustible materials should remain in place under the hearth or hearth extension after construction.

The inspector should inspect for hearths that are made of concrete or masonry. The inspector should inspect for hearths that have a thickness of less than 4 inches.

Fireplace Lintel

The lintel is located over the fireplace opening and supports the masonry above. It must be made of non-combustible material. The minimum bearing length of each end of the lintel is 4 inches.

Fireplace Size

The size of the fireplace is based on the size of the room. Most fireplaces are sized large enough to receive a 2-foot-long piece of firewood. With few design exceptions, the firebox of a concrete or masonry fireplace should be at least 20 inches deep.

Firebox Side and Rear Walls

The space inside the masonry fireplace is the combustion chamber or firebox. The firebox walls, which extend upward to the damper, could be made of solid masonry units, stone, and concrete.

If there's a lining of firebrick or other approved lining material inside the firebox, it should be at least 2 inches thick. Behind the lining should be the back and side walls made of solid masonry. The total thickness should be 8 inches, including the back wall and side walls, and the lining. The width of the mortar joints of the firebrick lining should not exceed 1/4-inch. The mortar is a special type of clay mortar used just for fireplace combustion chambers that can withstand excessive heat — a medium-duty refractory mortar.

If there's no lining inside the firebox, then the back and side walls should be at least 10 inches thick of solid masonry. Remember that this measurement is for masonry fireplaces and not factory-built fireplaces, which will be covered in the next section.

The firebox walls are slanted to reflect heat energy into the room. This angle of the walls is referred to as splay. Splay slope is usually 5 inches per foot. The sloped walls help direct smoke into the throat of the fireplace.

Fireplace Throat

The throat of the fireplace is located above the combustion chamber. It controls the efficiency of the fireplace. The rising smoke passes through the throat and enters the front side of the smoke chamber.

Fireplace Damper

Manually operated dampers can be installed only in connectors or chimneys serving solid fuel-burning fireplaces or stoves.

The damper is located above the fire and is used to control the combustion and prevent conditioned room air from escaping up the flue.

The damper must be made of a ferrous metal. The damper must be operable from the room containing the fireplace.

When there is smoke rising through the throat opening above the combustion chamber, the open damper is designed to control the downdraft. When hot gases and smoke rise up through the throat, they pass up into the front side of the smoke chamber. The rapid upward movement of the gases creates a downdraft on the rear side of the smoke chamber. One purpose of the opened damper door is to direct the downdraft back up into the smoke chamber and prevent it from pushing smoke into the room.

Fireplace Smoke Shelf

The smoke shelf is located behind the damper. It helps the open damper change the direction of the downdraft. A fireplace works well if the smoke shelf is deep. Some smoke shelves are curved.

Fireplace Smoke Chamber

The smoke chamber is located between the top of the throat to the bottom of the flue. Smoke would enter the room without a smoke chamber. Its size is large enough to hold a lot of smoke. The interior surfaces of the smoke chamber are usually sloped and coated with about a 1/2-inch-thick layer of cement mortar.

Fireplace Ash Dump

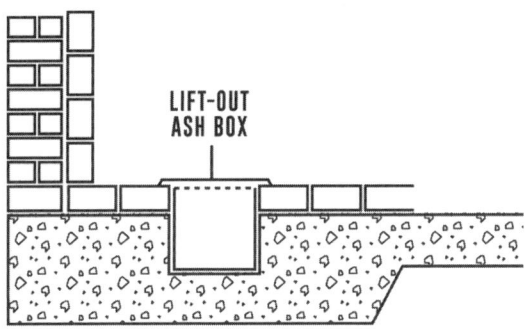

An ash dump is not required for every fireplace. It depends on the type of fireplace and foundation. Cleaning of the fireplace may be possible from the fireplace opening if it lacks an ash dump.

The ash dump is usually located in the rear hearth if there is an ash pit constructed below the fireplace. The ash dump is essentially an opening in the rear hearth through which ash and debris are passed. The ash dump is a pivoting metal door installed on a metal frame. The ash dump is typically made of cast iron. The homeowner generally cleans the fireplace by sweeping the cold ashes into the ash dump. The ashes fall downward and end up in the ash pit below. The ash pit must have a cleanout door.

If the house has a slab-on-grade foundation, the ash pit might not be as deep, but it would still require a cleanout of some type, usually accessed from the exterior. This design of having the fireplace cleanout door accessible from the exterior may be used when the fireplace is located on an outside wall.

For slab-on-grade foundations, a raised hearth will provide enough space for an ash pit under the fireplace. The cleanout door would have to be elevated high enough above grade in cold-weather climates to help prevent the door from being blocked by snow.

Ash Dump Cleanout

The cleanout for an ash dump must be made of ferrous metal, or a masonry door and frame built to stay tightly closed. An access for the cleanout door should be provided and made readily available so that the removal of ashes does not create a hazard.

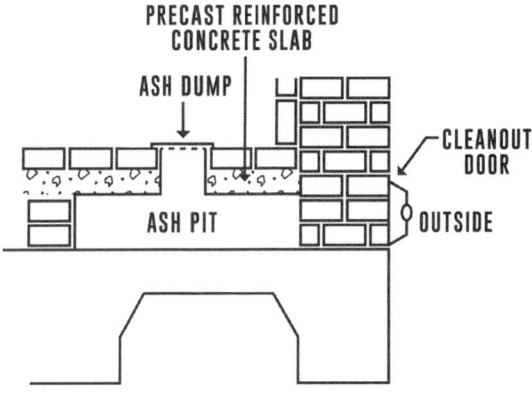

Masonry Chimney Cleanout

A masonry chimney cleanout is different from an ash dump cleanout. A masonry chimney cleanout is used to inspect, access, and clean the flue of a masonry chimney.

Below are photos from an inspection of a masonry chimney cleanout. This cleanout was opened, and debris was observed through the cleanout. Additionally, the upper edge of the cleanout opening was not at least 6 inches from the inlet. Corrections and further evaluations were needed.

A cleanout is not required if the masonry chimney is used for a fireplace where cleaning is possible through the fireplace's opening. An example of a required cleanout would be if the home had an oil-fired heating system that was connected to a masonry chimney.

At left is a photo of a masonry chimney cleanout for a fireplace. It shows an opened cleanout door for the ash dump. The ashes need to be cleaned out.

A cleanout for a masonry chimney should be made of non-combustible material. The cleanout opening for a masonry chimney must be located within 6 inches of the base of the flue. The upper edge of the cleanout should be at least 6 inches below the lowest inlet opening. And the cleanout opening should be at least 6 inches in height.

Exterior Air

Factory-built and masonry fireplaces must be provided with an exterior air supply to assure proper fuel combustion unless the room is mechanically ventilated.

The exterior air intake must supply all of the combustion air from the exterior of the dwelling, or from spaces within the dwelling ventilated with outside air, such as a ventilated crawlspace or ventilated attic space.

The exterior air intake must not be located within the garage or basement of the house.

Chimney Flue Size

The cross-sectional area of a chimney flue is based on the area of the fireplace opening. One rule of thumb is that the flue area should be at least one-tenth of the total fireplace opening.

Glass Doors

A glass door enclosure may be installed at a fireplace opening. The enclosure helps lessen the amount of heated room air that escapes up the chimney. The rate of combustion can be controlled with the glass doors and by adjusting the damper and draft vents that may also be installed.

Quiz #6

1. The smoke shelf is located behind the _____.

    ☐ damper
    ☐ flue connector pipe
    ☐ ash dump

2. T/F: One purpose of the opened damper door is to prevent the downdraft from pushing smoke into the room.

    ☐ True
    ☐ False

3. The damper must be operable from _____.

    ☐ the basement
    ☐ the room containing the fireplace
    ☐ under the hearth

4. T/F: The throat of the fireplace is located below the combustion chamber.

    ☐ True
    ☐ False

5. T/F: The throat of the fireplace controls the efficiency of the fireplace.

    ☐ True
    ☐ False

6. T/F: The fireplace firebox walls are slanted to reflect heat energy into the room.

    ☐ True
    ☐ False

7. T/F: The space inside the fireplace is called the firebox.

    ☐ True
    ☐ False

8. T/F: The size of the fireplace is based on the size of the room.

    ☐ True
    ☐ False

9. The _____ is located over the fireplace opening and supports the masonry above.

  ☐ lintel
  ☐ hearth
  ☐ flue lining

10. Fireplace hearths are typically made of _____.

  ☐ concrete or masonry
  ☐ wooden planks
  ☐ stainless steel

11. T/F: The back hearth is made up of compacted earth that can withstand heat from fire.

  ☐ True
  ☐ False

Answer Key is on page 74.

Factory-Built (Pre-Fabricated) Fireplaces

Factory-built or pre-fabricated fireplaces are found in many homes because they are less expensive to install than masonry fireplaces, and they come in a wide range of styles. Some factory-built fireplaces have a zero clearance requirement to combustibles, which means that the house's wooden framing can come into contact with the fireplace's components.

Factory-built fireplaces operate in the same way that masonry fireplaces do. They share the same components. Room air can enter a factory-built fireplace at the bottom of the unit near the floor, and wrap around the firebox through chambers. As the air is heated around the firebox, it flows upward. At the top of the factory-built fireplace, air registers allow the warm circulating air to exit and enter the room. Some fireplaces are equipped with circulating fans.

Factory-built fireplaces do not require a concrete foundation. Although most factory-built fireplaces are metal, pre-manufactured, modular, masonry fireplaces are also available. These masonry models incorporate special engineering techniques, including venting systems.

The image at right shows an exterior fresh-air intake for a pre-fabricated fireplace.

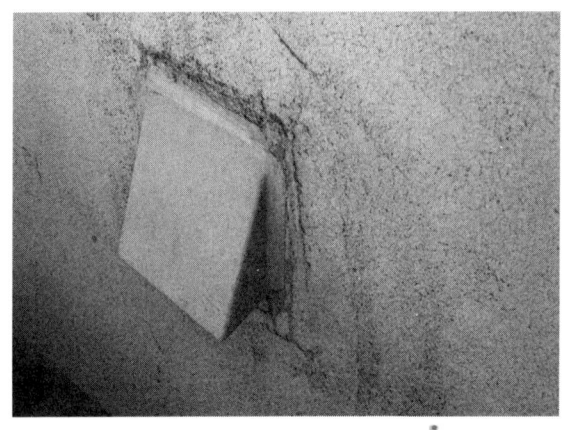

Factory-Built Chimneys

A factory-built chimney should be installed according to the manufacturer's instructions. All pre-fabricated chimneys must have a label from an approved agency that states the type of appliance with which the chimney was tested for use, a reference to the manufacturer's instructions, and the minimum clearances to combustibles. The manufacturer's instructions should contain every aspect of the installation of the chimney, including component assembly, clearances, supports, terminations, fire-blocking or fire stops, and connections.

Factory-built chimneys require no masonry construction. They're made of double- or triple-walled sections of metal pipe. Flanges and fittings are used to secure the fireplace and flue to the house's framing. Spacers provide proper clearances from combustible materials. The top of the factory-built chimney has a storm collar to divert rainwater from the chimney pipe to the chimney flashing. A chimney cap must be installed on top of the flue pipe.

If a factory-built chimney is used with a solid-fuel burner or an appliance with corrosive gases, the inside flue pipe should be made of stainless steel or have a porcelain-coated surface.

Chimneys for factory-built fireplaces require specific clearances and support components. The openings through the ceiling and roof should be carefully sized and constructed to provide the proper clearances. The openings through which the chimney passes should be blocked with fire-stop spacers and support boxes.

If the factory-built fireplace is located on an exterior wall, a chase can be constructed around the chimney to contain and protect it. The exterior walls of the chase are typically sided with the same exterior-covering materials as the rest of the house.

Panel Walls

The refractory panel walls of a factory-built fireplace require replacement if a nickel on its end can be inserted into the crack, or when the surface of the refractory panel has abraded more than 1/4-inch from the original surface. Replacement of the refractory panels should be completed by a qualified professional.

Quiz #7

1. If the factory-built fireplace is located on an exterior wall, a _____ can be constructed around the chimney to contain and protect it.

    ☐ run
    ☐ chase
    ☐ flue liner

2. T/F: Chimneys for factory-built fireplaces require specific clearances and support components.

    ☐ True
    ☐ False

3. T/F: The openings through which the chimneys of factory-built fireplaces pass should be blocked with fire-stop spacers and support boxes.

    ☐ True
    ☐ False

4. T/F: Factory-built chimneys are not required to be of masonry construction.

    ☐ True
    ☐ False

5. The top of a factory-built chimney has a _____ to divert rainwater from the chimney pipe to the chimney flashing.

    ☐ masonry stack
    ☐ storm collar
    ☐ damper door

6. A factory-built fireplace is _____ expensive to install than a masonry fireplace.

    ☐ more
    ☐ less

7. T/F: A factory-built fireplace has a zero clearance requirement to combustibles.

    ☐ True
    ☐ False

Answer Key is on page 75.

Wood-Burning Stoves

A wood-burning stove (also known as a wood stove) is a heating appliance made from iron or steel that is capable of burning wood fuel. Unlike a standard fireplace, a wood stove is typically contained entirely within the living space, rather than inset in a wall.

Wood stoves come in many different sizes, each suited for a different purpose.

Small stoves are suitable in single rooms, seasonal cottages, or small, energy-efficient homes. These models can also be used for zone heating in large homes where supplemental heating is needed.

Medium-size stoves are appropriate for heating small houses or mid-size homes that are intended to be energy-efficient and as inexpensive as possible to maintain.

Large stoves are used in larger homes or older homes that leak air and are located in colder climate zones.

To ensure safe and efficient use of wood-burning stoves, inspectors can pass along the following tips to their clients:

Never:

- burn coal. Coal burns significantly hotter than wood, posing a fire hazard.
- burn materials that will emit toxic chemicals, such as wood that has been pressure-treated or painted, colored paper, gift wrapping, plastic, plywood, particleboard, or questionable wood from furniture.
- burn wet wood. Generally speaking, it takes six months for cut, stored wood to dry out and be ready for use in wood-burning stoves.
- burn combustible liquids, such as kerosene, gasoline, alcohol or lighter fluid.
- let small children play near a lit wood-burning stove. Unlike standard fireplaces, whose sides are mostly inaccessible, all sides of wood stoves are exposed and capable of burning flesh or clothing.
- let the fire burn while the fire screen or door is open.

Always:

- use a grate to hold the logs so that they remain secured in the stove and the air can circulate adequately around them to keep the fire burning hot;
- keep the damper open while the stove is lit;
- dispose of ashes outdoors in a water-filled, metal container;
- check smoke alarms to make sure they are working properly; and
- periodically remove the stovepipe between the stove and the chimney so that it can be inspected for creosote. Homeowners may want to hire a professional to perform this service.

Efficiency and Air Pollutants

While federal and state governments crack down on vehicle and industrial emissions, they do relatively little to limit the harmful air pollution emitted from wood stoves. The problem is so bad that, in many areas, the smoke from wood stoves is the largest single contributor to local air pollution. Smoke from wood stoves can cause a variety of health ailments, from asthma to cancer.

To mitigate these concerns, the EPA sets requirements for wood-stove emissions based on the design of the stove: 4.1 grams of smoke per hour (g/h) for catalytic stoves, and 7.5 g/h for non-catalytic stoves. Some state laws further restrict airborne particulates, and many new models emit as little as 1 g/h.

These two approaches — catalytic and non-catalytic combustion — are described briefly as follows:

- In catalytic stoves, the smoky exhaust passes through a coated, ceramic honeycomb that ignites particulates and smoke gases. Catalysts degrade over time and must eventually be replaced, but they can last up to six seasons if the stove is used properly. Inadequate maintenance and the use of inappropriate fuel result in an early expiration of the catalyst. These stoves are typically more expensive than non-catalytic models, and they require more maintenance, although these challenges pay off through heightened efficiency.

- Non-catalytic stoves lack a catalyst but have three characteristics that assist in complete, clean combustion: pre-heated combustion air introduced from above the fuel; firebox insulation; and a large baffle to create hotter, longer air flow in the firebox. The baffle will eventually need to be replaced, as it deteriorates from combustion heat.

The following telltale signs indicate that the fire in a wood-burning stove suffers from oxygen deprivation and incomplete combustion, which will increase the emission of particulates into the air:

- It emits dark, smelly smoke. An efficient stove will produce little smoke.
- There is a smoky odor in the house.
- There is soot on the furniture.
- The stove is burning at less than 300° F. A flue pipe-mounted thermometer should read between 300° F and 400° F.
- The flames are dull and steady, rather than bright and lively.

To ensure efficiency, homeowners should follow these recommendations:

- Purchase a wood-burning stove listed by Underwriters Laboratories. Stoves tested by UL and other laboratories burn cleanly and efficiently.
- Burn only dry wood. Wood that has a moisture content (MC) of less than 20% burns hotter and cleaner than freshly cut wood, which may contain half of its weight in water.
- Burn hardwoods, such as oak, hickory and ash, once the fire has started. Softwoods, such as pine, ignite quicker and are excellent fire starters.
- Make sure the stove is properly sized for the space. Stoves that are too large for their area burn inefficiently.
- Burn smaller wood pieces rather than larger ones. Smaller pieces of wood have a large surface area, which allows them to burn hotter and cleaner.

In summary, a wood-burning stove, if properly designed and used appropriately for the space, is an efficient and clean way to heat a home.

Quiz 8

1. Wood that has a moisture content of less than _____% burns hotter and cleaner than freshly cut wood.

    ☐ 30
    ☐ 40
    ☐ 20

2. In _____ stoves, the smoky exhaust passes through a coated, ceramic honeycomb that ignites particulates and smoke gases.

    ☐ non-catalytic
    ☐ catalytic

3. _____ stoves have three characteristics that assist in complete, clean combustion: pre-heated combustion air introduced from above the fuel; firebox insulation; and a large baffle.

    ☐ Catalytic
    ☐ Non-catalytic

4. _____ from wood stoves can cause a variety of health ailments, from asthma to cancer.

    ☐ Smoke
    ☐ Ashes
    ☐ Odor

5. T/F: It is safe to burn coal in a wood stove.

    ☐ True
    ☐ False

6. T/F: It is safe to dispose of ashes from a wood stove using a central vacuum system.

    ☐ True
    ☐ False

7. T/F: Homeowners should periodically remove the stovepipe between the stove and the chimney so that it can be inspected for creosote.

    ☐ True
    ☐ False

Answer Key is on page 75.

Initial Inspection

The inspector should inspect for the following:

- solid fuel-burning appliances or fireplaces improperly located where gasoline or other flammable vapors or gases are present;
- any unused openings in chimneys or flues;
- the lack of a smoke detector. A smoke detector should be installed in the same room as the fireplace; and
- the lack of a carbon-monoxide detector. A carbon-monoxide detector should be installed in the same room as the fireplace.

Fireplaces

The inspector should inspect for the following hazardous conditions:

- a combustible lintel above the fireplace opening;
- combustible material within 6 inches above the fireplace opening that projects out 1½ inches or less from the face of the fireplace;
- combustible material within 12 inches above a fireplace opening that projects out more than 1½ inches from the face of the fireplace;
- a throat or damper located less than 8 inches above the fireplace opening;
- a manually operated damper that does not operate or close properly; and
- a damper or damper component that has rust or corrosion.

Hearths, Hearth Extensions and Fire Chambers

The inspector should inspect for hearths that:

- are not made of concrete or masonry; and
- have a thickness of less than 4 inches.

The inspector should inspect for hearth extensions that:

- have a thickness of less than 2 inches;
- are less than 16 inches in front of or less than 8 inches beyond each side of the fireplace opening (6 square feet or less); and
- are less than 20 inches in front of or less than 12 inches beyond each side of the fireplace opening (greater than 6 square feet).

The inspector should inspect hearths, hearth extensions, and chambers for joint separation, damage and deterioration.

Inspection of Single-Wall Metal Chimney

The inspector should inspect for single-wall metal chimneys in one- and two-family dwellings. Single-wall metal chimneys should not be used in one- and two-family dwellings.

The inspector should inspect for wall protectors (heat shields) with less than a 1-inch air gap.

Interior Single-Wall Metal Chimneys

The inspector should inspect for exposed interior single-wall metal chimneys that are not continuously enclosed where they extend through closets, storage areas, or habitable spaces, or where the surface of the chimney could come into contact with people or combustible materials.

The inspector should inspect for interior single-wall metal chimneys:

- for distances less than 18 inches away from wood-framed walls or combustible materials;
- sized 18 inches or under in diameter that are less than 2 inches away from non-combustible walls; and
- sized more than 18 inches in diameter that are less than 4 inches away from non-combustible walls.

Exterior Single-Wall Metal Chimneys

The inspector should inspect for distances between exterior-mounted, single-wall metal chimneys:

- that are less than 2 feet away from doors, windows or walkways;
- that are less than 18 inches away from wood-framed walls or combustible materials;
- sized 18 inches or under in diameter that are less than 2 inches away from non-combustible walls; and
- sized over 18 inches in diameter that are less than 4 inches away from non-combustible walls.

Chimney Outlets

The inspector should inspect for missing thimbles where chimneys pass through combustible roofs.

The inspector should inspect for chimneys that terminate less than:

- 3 feet above the highest point where they pass through the roof surface;
- 2 feet above any portion of a building within 10 feet;
- 3 feet from adjacent buildings or building openings; or
- 10 feet above grade or walkways.

The inspector should inspect for chimney outlets that jeopardize people's safety, overheat combustible structures, or that might cause flue gases to enter nearby building openings

Initial Inspection

The inspector should inspect the crowns of masonry chimneys for slopes that direct water into flues.

Flues and Liners

The inspector should inspect for galvanized flues and connectors. Flues and connectors should not be galvanized.

The inspector should inspect readily accessible and visible flues for rust and corrosion.

The inspector should inspect for masonry chimneys that are not lined. All masonry chimneys should be lined.

The inspector should inspect for linings that don't extend the entire length of the chimney to a level of 4 inches or more above the masonry cap (crown, splay or wash).

The inspector should inspect for liners that are visibly softened, cracked, deteriorated or damaged.

The inspector should inspect readily accessible and visible flues and liners for excessive accumulation of creosote, soot, or other combustible material.

The inspector should inspect for flues that have two or more openings at the same level.

The inspector should inspect for venting into the space around and between liners. The remaining space surrounding a chimney liner should not be used as a vent.

Flue Size

The inspector should inspect the size of the flue, if visible, and compare it to the size of the fireplace opening. This relationship is the most important factor in achieving sufficient draft. A flue that is too small relative to the fireplace opening will be unable to lift and remove hazardous flue gases to the outside.

Maximum Fireplace Opening for Round Flues	
Round Flues	Maximum Fireplace Opening
4 inches in diameter	150 square inches
5 inches in diameter	235 square inches
6 inches in diameter	339 square inches
7 inches in diameter	461 square inches
8 inches in diameter	603 square inches

Maximum Fireplace Opening for Round Flues	
Round Flues	Maximum Fireplace Opening
9 inches in diameter	763 square inches
10 inches in diameter	942 square inches
11 inches in diameter	1,140 square inches
12 inches in diameter	1,357 square inches
13 inches in diameter	1,592 square inches
14 inches in diameter	1,847 square inches
15 inches in diameter	2,120 square inches
16 inches in diameter	2,412 square inches
17 inches in diameter	2,723 square inches
18 inches in diameter	3,053 square inches
19 inches in diameter	3,402 square inches
20 inches in diameter	3,769 square inches
21 inches in diameter	4,156 square inches
22 inches in diameter	4,561 square inches
23 inches in diameter	4,985 square inches
24 inches in diameter	5,428 square inches
25 inches in diameter	5,890 square inches
26 inches in diameter	6,371 square inches
27 inches in diameter	6,870 square inches
28 inches in diameter	7,389 square inches
29 inches in diameter	7,926 square inches
30 inches in diameter	8,482 square inches

Maximum Fireplace Opening, in Square Inches, for Rectangular Flues

Find the maximum size of the fireplace opening by matching the flue dimensions to the left column and top row of chart.

	6"	7"	8"	9"	10"	11"	12"	13"	14"	15"	16"	17"	18"	19"	20"	21"	22"	23"	24"	25"	26"	27"	28"
4"	240	280	256	288	320	352	384	416	448	480	512	544	576	608	640	672	704	736	768	800	832	864	896
5"	300	350	400	450	400	440	480	520	560	600	640	680	720	760	800	840	880	920	960	1000	1040	1080	1120
6"	360	420	480	540	600	660	576	624	672	720	768	816	864	912	960	1008	1056	1104	1152	1200	1248	1296	1344
7"	420	490	560	630	700	770	840	910	784	840	896	952	1008	1064	1120	1176	1232	1288	1344	1400	1456	1512	1568
8"	480	560	640	720	800	880	960	1040	1120	1200	1024	1088	1152	1216	1280	1344	1408	1472	1536	1600	1664	1728	1792
9"	540	630	720	810	900	990	1080	1170	1260	1350	1440	1530	1296	1368	1440	1512	1584	1656	1728	1800	1872	1944	2016
10"	600	700	800	900	1000	1100	1200	1300	1400	1500	1600	1700	1700	1900	1600	1680	1760	1840	1920	2000	2080	2160	2240
11"	660	770	880	990	1100	1210	1320	1430	1540	1650	1760	1870	1980	2090	2200	2310	1936	2024	2112	2200	2288	2376	2464
12"	576	840	960	1080	1200	1320	1440	1560	1680	1800	1920	2040	2160	2280	2400	2520	2640	2760	2304	2400	2496	2592	2688
13"	624	910	1040	1170	1300	1430	1560	1690	1820	1950	2080	2210	2340	2470	2600	2730	2860	2990	3120	3250	2704	2808	2912
14"	672	784	1120	1260	1400	1540	1680	1820	1960	2100	2240	2380	2520	2660	2800	2940	3080	3220	3360	3500	3640	3780	3136
15"	720	840	1200	1350	1500	1650	1800	1950	2100	2250	2400	2550	2700	2850	3000	3150	3300	3450	3600	3750	3900	4050	4200
16"	768	896	1024	1440	1600	1760	1920	2080	2240	2400	2560	2720	2880	3040	3200	3360	3520	3680	3840	4000	4160	4320	4480
17"	816	952	1088	1530	1700	1870	2040	2210	2380	2550	2720	2890	3060	3230	3400	3570	3740	3910	4080	4250	4420	4590	4760
18"	864	1008	1152	1296	1800	1980	2160	2340	2520	2700	2880	3060	3240	3420	3600	3780	3960	4140	4320	4500	4680	4860	5040
19"	912	1064	1216	1368	1900	2090	2280	2470	2660	2850	3040	3230	3420	3610	3800	3990	4180	4370	4560	4750	4940	5130	5320
20"	960	1120	1280	1440	1600	2200	2400	2600	2800	3000	3200	3400	3600	3800	4000	4200	4400	4600	4800	5000	5200	5400	5600
21"	1008	1176	1344	1512	1680	2310	2520	2730	2940	3150	3360	3570	3780	3990	4200	4410	4620	4830	5040	5250	5460	5670	5880
22"	1056	1232	1408	1584	1760	1936	2640	2860	3080	3300	3520	3740	3960	4180	4400	4620	4840	5060	5280	5500	5720	5940	6160
23"	1104	1288	1472	1656	1840	2024	2760	2990	3220	3450	3680	3910	4140	4370	4600	4830	5060	5290	5520	5750	5980	6210	6440
24"	1152	1344	1536	1728	1920	2112	2304	3120	3360	3600	3840	4080	4320	4560	4800	5040	5280	5520	5760	6000	6240	6480	6720
25"	1200	1400	1600	1800	2000	2200	2400	3250	3500	3750	4000	4250	4500	4750	5000	5250	5500	5750	6000	6250	6500	6750	7000
26"	1248	1456	1664	2080	2288	2496	2496	2704	3640	3900	4160	4420	4680	4940	5200	5460	5720	5980	6240	6500	6760	7020	7280
27"	1296	1512	1728	1944	2160	2376	2592	2808	3780	4050	4320	4590	4860	5130	5400	5670	5940	6210	6480	6750	7020	7290	7560
28"	1344	1568	1792	2016	2240	2464	2688	2912	3136	4200	4480	4760	5040	5320	5600	5880	6160	6440	6720	7000	7280	7560	7840
29"	1392	1624	1856	2088	2320	2552	2784	3016	3248	4350	4640	4930	5220	5510	5800	6090	6380	6670	6960	7250	7540	7830	8120
30"	1440	1680	1920	2160	2400	2640	2880	3120	3360	3600	4800	5100	5400	5700	6000	6300	6600	6900	7200	7500	7800	8100	8400

Connectors

The inspector should inspect for connectors from solid fuel-burning appliances that have a rise to the chimney of less than 1/4-inch per foot.

The inspector should inspect for connectors:

- that are not as short or straight as possible;
- that are covered with insulation; and
- of natural-draft appliances connected to the positive pressure-side of a mechanical draft system.

The inspector should inspect for the improper installation of larger connector pipes entering a flue above smaller connector pipes. The smaller appliance vent connector should connect to the chimney above the larger one. If there are two or more vent connectors entering a common gas vent, chimney flue, or single-wall metal pipe, the smaller vent connector pipe must enter the vent, flue or pipe at the highest point allowed. If there are two or more vent connector pipes entering one chimney flue or vent, the pipe penetrations must be at different levels, or the connectors must be installed at an angle of 45 degrees or less relative to the vertical.

Vent connectors for Category I appliances should not be connected to any vent connector pipe of a mechanical draft system operating under positive static pressure.

Below is an illustration of two appliances and their vent connectors entering the same chimney flue. The smaller vent connector pipe is higher than the larger one.

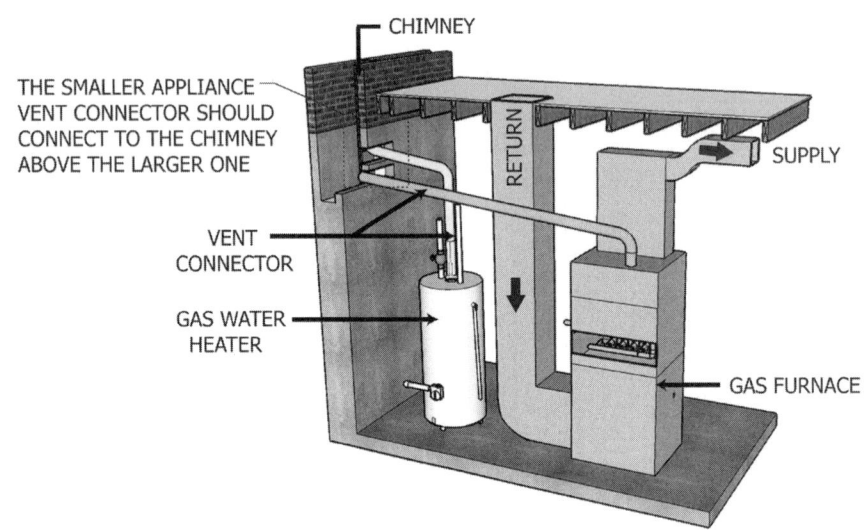

CHIMNEY/VENT CONNECTIONS

Cleanouts

The inspector should inspect cleanouts for doors and frames that are not made of ferrous metal, pre-cast cement, or other non-combustible material.

The inspector should inspect combustible materials projecting beyond the faces of chimneys that are within 18 inches of cleanout openings.

Initial Inspection

The inspector should inspect for combustible materials stored within 18 inches of cleanout doors.

The inspector should inspect cleanout doors that are obstructed or do not close tightly.

The inspector should inspect the interior cleanout's lower edge for heights above the lowest accessible floor level that are less than 16 inches.

The inspector should inspect the exterior cleanout's lower edge for heights above grade that are less than 16 inches.

The inspector should inspect the bases of fireplace chimney flues for distances that are not between 6 and 12 inches below the bottom edges of their cleanout openings.

Preventing Chimney Collapse

Chimneys are among the heaviest and most structurally vulnerable of all exterior components of a building. Accidents caused by their collapse can lead to death. A collapse can also cause costly structural damage to the building and its surroundings. Inspection, maintenance and preparedness are critical safeguards against chimney collapse.

Wind and other elements may cause an already weakened chimney to collapse. An elderly man in Britain was crushed by a wind-toppled chimney as it fell from the roof of the managed-care facility where he lived. This case is, unfortunately, fairly unremarkable, as such accidents occur often for a variety of reasons—from weathering and wind, to falling tree limbs and poor design.

Chimneys collapse by the hundreds during major earthquakes, typically snapping at the roofline. More than half of the homes in Washington state inspected by the Federal Emergency Management Agency (FEMA) following the Nisqually Earthquake in 2001 sustained chimney damage. Chimney collapses were widely reported following the massive 7.1-magnitude earthquake that struck New Zealand in September 2010.

Earthquake damage and injuries can be caused, in large part, by bricks and stones as they fall from chimneys onto vehicles, structures, and people. These collapses happen suddenly and without warning. Collapses can also cause implosion-type destruction as the chimney makes its way through the roof and attic, demolishing part of the living space and injuring occupants below. For these reasons, it is crucial that chimneys, especially in seismically active regions, be inspected periodically for signs of weakening. Following an earthquake, it is even more vital that chimneys be inspected for indications of imminent or future collapse.

Chimneys should be inspected for the following defects:

- mortar between the bricks or stones that crumbles when poked with a screwdriver;
- missing or insufficient lateral support (such as steel straps) used to tie the chimney to the structure at the roof and floor levels. Building codes in some seismically active regions require internal and external bracing of chimneys to the structure;

- mechanical damage to the chimney, such as that caused by falling tree limbs or scaffolding;
- visible tilting or separation from the building. Any gap should be frequently measured to monitor whether it is increasing; and
- chimney footing defects, including the following:
    - undersized footing, which is footing cast so thin that it breaks, or does not sufficiently extend past the chimney's base to support its weight;
    - deteriorated footing, caused by weathering, frost, loose or poor-quality construction; and
    - poor soil below the footing, including eroded, settled, or otherwise weakened soil, frost heaving, or expansive clay beneath the footing.

A more thorough inspection performed to the International Phase I Standards of Practice for Inspecting Fireplaces and Chimneys may also be considered.

The following additional precautions may be taken:

- Attach plywood panels to the roof or above the ceiling joists to act as a barrier between falling masonry and the roof.
- Strengthen the existing chimney by repairing weak areas.
- Tear down the chimney and replace it with a flue or a stronger chimney. Keep in mind that tall, slender, masonry chimneys are the most vulnerable to earthquakes, weathering, and other forms of wear. However, even newer reinforced or metal flue chimneys can sustain significant damage and require repair.
- Relocate children's play areas, patios, and parking areas away from a damaged chimney.
- Instruct family members to get away from chimneys during earthquakes.

Homeowners should contact their local building departments to obtain required permits before starting any significant construction that may affect the chimney structure and/or its supports.

In addition to collapse hazards, leaning chimneys can also make using the fireplace dangerous. Hearth cracks, side cracks in the fireplace, openings around the fireplace, and chimney damage all present the risk that sparks or smoke will enter the living space or building cavities. Check for evidence of fireplace movement. Following an earthquake, homeowners should have their chimney inspected before using the fireplace.

Commercial chimney collapses are rare, but they deserve mention due to the devastation they cause. In one terrible incident in central India, more than 100 workers were killed when a 900-foot tall chimney collapsed on a construction site. One of the worst construction site disasters in recent history, the collapse was blamed on heavy rain. While safety standards are generally more stringent outside of India, commercial chimneys everywhere require inspection.

In summary, chimneys should be inspected to prevent expensive and potentially deadly collapses.

Quiz #9

1. T/F: The inspector should inspect cleanouts for doors and frames that are not made of ferrous metal, pre-cast cement, or other non-combustible material.

    ☐ True
    ☐ False

2. T/F: The inspector should inspect for connectors from solid fuel-burning appliances that have a rise to the chimney of less than 1/4-inch per foot.

    ☐ True
    ☐ False

3. T/F: Flue and connector pipes should be galvanized.

    ☐ True
    ☐ False

4. T/F: The inspector should inspect for flues that have two or more openings at the same level.

    ☐ True
    ☐ False

5. The inspector should inspect for chimneys that terminate less than ___ feet above the highest point where they pass through the roof surface.

    ☐ 2
    ☐ 1
    ☐ 3

6. T/F: Single-wall metal chimneys should always be used in one- and two-family dwellings.

    ☐ True
    ☐ False

7. T/F: The inspector should inspect for hearths that are not made of concrete or masonry.

    ☐ True
    ☐ False

8. T/F: The inspector should inspect for combustible lintels above fireplace openings.

    ☐ True
    ☐ False

Answer Key is on page 75.

Water Damage

All masonry and factory-built fireplaces and chimneys can be adversely affected by direct contact with water. All chimneys can deteriorate from prolonged contact with water. Masonry materials deteriorate quickly when exposed to the freeze/thaw process, during which moisture that has penetrated the materials periodically freezes and expands, causing undue stress. Water can also cause rust in steel and cast iron.

The inspector should look for:

- efflorescence;
- rusted dampers;
- deteriorated masonry;
- rusted or corroded metal;
- wood rot at nearby framing;
- water stains;
- clogged cleanout;
- deteriorated mortar joints;
- a cracked flue lining;
- a damaged hearth;
- a tilted chimney stack; and
- settlement cracks.

Chimney Deterioration Due to Condensation

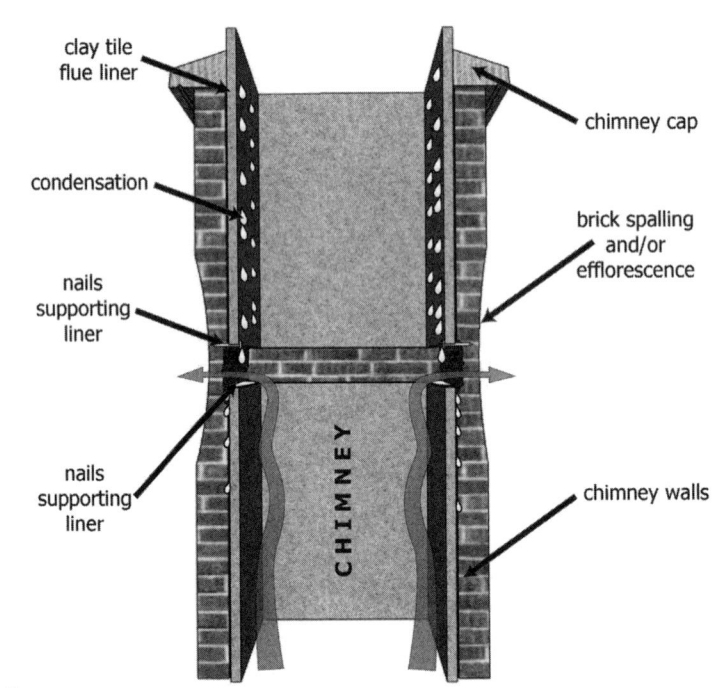

Water-Damaged Mortar Joints

Water can easily penetrate deteriorated mortar joints on the chimneys. Deteriorated mortar joints can appear cracked, weathered away, and have loose chunks of material. A common repair for deteriorated mortar joints is called repointing, where the existing mortar joint is cut out and the joint is re-packed with new mortar.

Install a Cricket to Stop or Prevent Leaks

If the chimney is located on the low side of a roof where water runoff is directed against it, the installation of a cricket will afford additional protection against water leaking into the home. A cricket is a water deflector that serves to direct rainwater away from the chimney. A cricket is recommended for a chimney that's more than 30 inches wide. Crickets are especially important for chimneys on steep roofs.

Indications of an active roof leak can be seen at the chimney flashing area, as observed in the unfinished attic space pictured at left.

Efflorescence

Efflorescence is the white chalky powder that you might find on the surface of a concrete or brick wall. It can be a cosmetic issue, or it can be an indication of moisture intrusion that could lead to major structural and indoor air quality issues. A home inspector should understand what efflorescence is in order to recognize potential moisture problems.

Identifying Efflorescence

InterNACHI® inspectors should already know how to distinguish mold from efflorescence (see image below), but it is possible for homeowners to confuse the two. The expense of a mold test can be avoided if the substance in question can be identified as efflorescence.

Here are a few tips that inspectors can offer their clients so that they understand the differences:

- Pinched between the fingers, efflorescence will turn into a powder, while mold will not.
- Efflorescence forms on inorganic building materials, while mold forms on organic substances. However, it is possible for mold to consume dirt on brick or cement.
- Efflorescence will dissolve in water, while mold will not.
- Efflorescence is almost always white, yellow or brown, while mold can be any color imaginable. If the substance in question is purple, pink or black, it is not efflorescence.
- Efflorescence has a salty taste.

Aside from mold, the following conditions can result from excess moisture in a residence:

- fungi that rot wood;
- water damage to sheetrock; and
- reduced effectiveness of insulation.

Inspectors should note in their inspection reports the presence of efflorescence because it generally occurs where there is excess moisture, a condition that also encourages mold growth.

Prevention and Removal of Efflorescence

Prevention

- An impregnating hydrophobic sealant can be applied to a surface to prevent the unwanted intrusion of water. It will also prevent water from traveling to the surface from within. In cold climates, this sealant can cause material to break during freeze/thaw cycles.
- During home construction, bricks left out overnight should be kept on pallets and be covered. Moisture from damp soil and rain can be absorbed into the brick.
- Install capillary breaks, including polyethelene sheeting between the soil and the building material, such as concrete.

Removal

- Pressurized water can sometimes be used to remove or dissolve efflorescence.
- An acid, such as diluted muriatic acid, can be used to dissolve efflorescence. Water should be applied first so that the acid does not discolor the brick. Following application, baking soda can be used to neutralize the acid and prevent any additional damage to the masonry. Muriatic acid is toxic, and contact with skin or eyes should be avoided.
- A strong brush can be used to simply scrub the efflorescence off.

Note: The use of water to remove efflorescence may result in the re-absorption of crystals into the host material. If water is used in the removal process, the material should be dried off very quickly to prevent efflorescence from re-forming.

In summary, efflorescence is a cosmetic issue, but it indicates a potential moisture problem. Inspectors should know how capillary forces can cause structural damage to building materials, and educate their clients about efflorescence and the potential problems it may cause.

Porous Building Materials

Building materials, such as concrete, wood, brick and stone, are porous materials. Porous materials can absorb or wick water by a process called the capillary action. As water moves through the porous material, salts can be drawn with it.

Concrete, wood, brick, stone and mortar are porous materials that contain salts. The ground that these materials can come into contact with also contains salts. Capillary action can literally suck water and transport it through porous building materials.

Capillary Action

Porous building materials are capable of wicking water for large distances due to capillary action with a theoretical limit of capillary rise of about 6 miles. That's 6 miles directly up. Think of a tree and how a tree can transport water from its roots to its leaves. That's capillary action. And it's very powerful. When you add salt to that capillary process, it can be destructive.

Salts dissolved by groundwater can be transported by capillary action through porous soil. Building materials in contact with soil will naturally wick the water inward and upward. Take concrete footings—they are typically poured directly onto soil without any capillary break. Sometimes this is called rising damp. This is the beginning of how water can wick upward into a structure.

Destructive Pressures

When the capillary flow of water reaches the surface of a building material, evaporation occurs. As the water evaporates, salt is left behind. As this evaporation of capillary flow continues, the salt concentration increases through the process of osmosis, which creates an imbalance. Nature abhors imbalance and always wants to put things back into equilibrium. To re-establish equilibrium through osmosis, water rushes toward the salt deposit to dilute the concentration. This rush of water creates massive hydrostatic pressures within the porous material, and these pressures are destructive.

The pressure from osmosis can create incredibly strong hydrostatic pressure that can exceed the strength of building materials, including concrete.

Here are some examples of how that pressure translates:

- Diffusion vapor pressure: 0.3 to 0.5 psi
- Capillary pressure: 300 to 500 psi
- Osmotic pressure: 3,000 to 5,000 psi

As you can see from the list above, osmosis can create pressure that is greater than the structural strength of concrete, which can be from 2,000 psi to 3,000 psi. The action of water rushing to the surface due to capillary action creates incredible forces that can cause materials to flake, crack, and break apart.

Spalling

When efflorescence leads to strong osmotic pressures—greater than the strength of the building material—and the material literally breaks apart, the resulting damage is called spalling. Hydrostatic pressure can cause spalling, but spalling can also be caused by freeze-thaw cycles in building materials that have a high moisture content.

Both efflorescence and spalling can be prevented with capillary breaks, such as by installing a polyethylene sheeting under a concrete slab.

Chimney Kickout Flashing

Kickout flashing, also known as diverter flashing, is a special type of flashing that diverts rainwater away from the cladding and into the gutter. When installed properly, it provides excellent protection against the penetration of water into the building envelope.

Several factors can lead to rainwater intrusion, but a missing kickout flashing, in particular, often results in concentrated areas of water accumulation and potentially severe damage to exterior walls. InterNACHI® inspectors should make sure that kickouts are present where they are needed, and that they are installed correctly.

Water penetration into the cladding can occasionally be observed on the exterior wall in the form of vertical water stains, although inspectors should not rely on visual identification. There may be severe damage with little or no visible evidence.

Inspectors may observe the following problems associated with kickout flashing:

1. The kickout was never installed.

   - The need for kickout flashing was developed fairly recently, and the builder may not have been aware that one was required. The increased amount of insulation and building wrap that is used in modern construction makes buildings less breathable and more likely to sustain water damage. Kickout flashing prevents rainwater from being absorbed into the wall, making it more essential than ever.

   The following are locations where kickout flashing installation is critical:

   - anywhere a roof and exterior wall intersect, where the wall continues past the lower roof-edge and gutter. If a kickout flashing is absent in these locations, large amounts of water may miss the gutter, penetrate the siding, and become trapped inside the wall; and
   - where gutters terminate at the side of a chimney.

2. The kickout was improperly installed.

   - The bottom seam of the flashing must be watertight. If it's not, water will leak through the seam and may penetrate the cladding.
   - The angle of the diverter should never be less than 110 degrees.

3. The kick-out was modified by the homeowner.

   - Homeowners who do not understand the importance of kickouts may choose to alter them because they are unsightly. A common way this is done is to shorten their height to less than the standard 6 inches (although some manufacturers permit 4 inches), which will greatly reduce their effectiveness. Kickout flashings should be the same height as the side wall flashings.
   - Homeowners may also make kickout flashings less conspicuous by cutting them flush with the wall, making them less effective.

In summary, kickout flashing should be present and properly installed in order to direct rainwater away from the exterior roof-covering materials, particularly at the chimney locations.

International Phase I Standards of Practice for Inspecting Fireplaces and Chimneys

17.1 About These Standards for Inspecting Fireplaces and Chimneys

Although this Standard applies to both commercial and residential fireplaces and chimneys, it exceeds the requirements of both InterNACHI's Commercial and Residential Standards of Practices. The inspection shall include examination of readily accessible and visible portions of solid fuel-burning, low-heat fireplaces and chimneys.

17.2 Purpose

The purpose of this document is to establish international standards for the inspection of fireplaces and chimneys. This document also provides universal fireplace and chimney inspection reporting language.

17.3 Definitions

17.3.1 Fireplace and Chimney-Specific Definitions

- **accessible:** in the opinion of the inspector, can be approached or entered safely without difficulty, fear or danger.
- **chimney:** a structure containing one or more flues for removing gases to the outside atmosphere.
- **cleanout:** an opening in a chimney that provides access to the flue for cleaning purposes.
- **clearance:** the minimum distance through air measured between the surface of something heat-producing and the surface of something combustible.
- **connector:** the pipe that connects a fuel-burning appliance to a chimney.
- **crown:** the sloped top of a masonry chimney designed to shed water away from the flue; also called a **splay** or **wash**.
- **damper:** a manually operated plate for controlling the draft in the flue.
- **fireplace lintel:** a horizontal, non-combustible member that spans the top of the fireplace opening.
- **flue:** a passage through which gases move from the fire chamber to the outer air.
- **hearth:** the floor within a fireplace.
- **hearth extension:** non-combustible material in front of and at the sides of a fireplace opening.
- **mantel:** a shelf or horizontal ornament above a fireplace opening.
- **Phase I:** a type of fireplace and chimney inspection that exceeds the standards required by a standard home inspection.
- **single-wall metal chimney:** a field-constructed chimney not permitted in one- and two-family dwellings.

fuel: wood, coal, pellets, and other materials that can be burned for heat.

thimble: the tube or lining through a wall that a connector passes through to enter a flue, or that a flue passes through to exit a roof.

- **wall protector:** a non-combustible shield between a wall and anything heat-producing for the purpose of reducing the required clearance.

17.3.2 Terminology Commonly Found in Commercial Property Inspection Reports

Visit **www.nachi.org/comsop.htm#101**

17.4 Goal of the Inspection

The goal of the inspection is to provide observations that may lead to the decrease of hazardous conditions associated with fireplaces and chimneys.

17.5 Limitations

The inspection is limited to the readily accessible and visible portions of the fireplace and chimney. The inspection should not be considered all-inclusive or technically exhaustive.

This Standard does not require the inspector to:

- inspect appliances, wall furnaces, stoves, water heaters, incinerators, mechanical draft systems, draft regulators, catalytic converters, pollution-control devices, heat-reclamation devices, spark arrestors, induced-draft chimneys, fire-stopping, or for condensation issues.
- determine fire rating, adequacy of combustion air, status of product listing, compliance with manufacturers' instructions, proper clearances, proper load paths, combustibility, proper placement of flue size changes, proper thimble installation, or repair history.
- remove or inspect fireplace inserts, stoves or accessories.
- determine the need for fire-stopping, chimney enclosures, hearth thickness mitigation, or seismic reinforcing.
- test smoke detectors or carbon-monoxide detectors.
- perform video scans, smoke tests, flue-gas measurements, or engineering calculations.

These Standards do not apply to the inspection of mobile homes.

17.6 Optional Add-On Inspection Service

Although InterNACHI's Standards of Practice for Inspecting Commercial Properties and InterNACHI's Standards of Practice for Performing a General Home Inspection do not require the inspector to perform a Phase I Fireplace and Chimney Inspection, it may be offered in conjunction with a complete commercial or residential property inspection, or as a separate, stand-alone inspection service.

17.7 Inspection Frequency

The inspector should advise his/her client that all fireplaces and chimneys should be inspected

International Phase I Standards of Practice for Inspecting Fireplaces

prior to their first use, and not less than annually.

17.8 Visual Inspection

17.8.1 Initial Inspection

    17.8.1.1 The inspector should inspect for solid fuel-burning appliances or fireplaces improperly located where gasoline or other flammable vapors or gases are present.

    17.8.1.2 The inspector should inspect for unused openings in chimneys and flues.

    17.8.1.3 The inspector should inspect for lack of a smoke detector. A smoke detector should be installed in the same room as the fireplace.

    17.8.1.4 The inspector should inspect for lack of a carbon-monoxide detector. A carbon-monoxide detector should be installed in the same room as the fireplace.

17.8.2 Fireplaces

    17.8.2.1 The inspector should inspect for combustible lintels above fireplace openings.

    17.8.2.2 The inspector should inspect for combustible material within 6 inches above fireplace openings that projects out 1½ inches or less from the face of the fireplace.

    17.8.2.3 The inspector should inspect for combustible material within 12 inches above fireplace openings that projects out more than 1½ inches from the face of the fireplace.

    17.8.2.4 The inspector should inspect for throats or dampers located less than 8 inches above fireplace openings.

    17.8.2.5 The inspector should inspect for manually operated dampers that do not operate or close properly.

    17.8.2.6 The inspector should inspect for dampers and damper components that have rust or corrosion.

17.8.3 Hearths, Hearth Extensions and Fire Chambers

    17.8.3.1 The inspector should inspect for hearth extensions that have a thickness of less than 2 inches.

    17.8.3.2 The inspector should inspect for hearth extensions that are less than 16 inches in front of or less than 8 inches beyond each side of the fireplace openings (6 square feet or less).

    17.8.3.3 The inspector should inspect for hearth extensions that are less than 20 inches in front of or less than 12 inches beyond each side of the fireplace openings (greater than 6 square feet).

    17.8.3.4 The inspector should inspect the hearth, hearth extension and chambers for joint separation, damage and deterioration.

17.8.4 Single-Wall Metal Chimneys

17.8.4.1 Initial Single-Wall Metal Chimney Inspection

17.8.4.1.1 The inspector should inspect for single-wall metal chimneys in one- and two-family dwellings. Single-wall metal chimneys should not be used in one- and two-family dwellings.

17.8.4.1.2 The inspector should inspect for wall protectors (heat shields) with less than 1-inch air gaps.

17.8.4.2 Interior Single-Wall Metal Chimneys

17.8.4.2.1 The inspector should inspect for exposed interior single-wall metal chimneys that are not continuously enclosed where they extend through closets, storage areas, or habitable spaces, or where the surface of a chimney could come into contact with people or combustible materials.

17.8.4.2.2 The inspector should inspect for interior single-wall metal chimneys for distances of less than 18 inches from wood-framed walls or combustible materials.

17.8.4.2.3 The inspector should inspect for interior single-wall metal chimneys 18 inches or under in diameter that are less than 2 inches from non-combustible walls.

17.8.4.2.4 The inspector should inspect for interior single-wall metal chimneys over 18 inches in diameter that are less than 4 inches from non-combustible walls.

17.8.4.3 Exterior Single-Wall Metal Chimneys

17.8.4.3.1 The inspector should inspect for distances between exterior-mounted, single-wall metal chimneys that are less than 2 feet from doors, windows or walkways.

17.8.4.3.2 The inspector should inspect for distances between exterior-mounted, single-wall metal chimneys that are less than 18 inches from wood-framed walls or combustible materials.

17.8.4.3.3 The inspector should inspect for distances between exterior-mounted, single-wall metal chimneys 18 inches or under in diameter that are less than 2 inches from non-combustible walls.

17.8.4.3.4 The inspector should inspect for distances between exterior-mounted, single-wall metal chimneys over 18 inches in diameter that are less than 4 inches from non-combustible walls.

17.8.5 Chimney Outlets

17.8.5.1 The inspector should inspect for missing ventilating thimbles where chimneys pass through combustible roofs.

17.8.5.2 The inspector should inspect for chimneys that terminate less than 3 feet above the highest point where they pass through the roof surface.

17.8.5.3 The inspector should inspect for chimneys that terminate less than 2 feet above any portion of a building (ridge, wall or parapet) within 10 feet.

17.8.5.4 The inspector should inspect for chimneys that terminate less than 3 feet from adjacent buildings or building openings.

17.8.5.5 The inspector should inspect for chimneys that terminate less than 10 feet above grade or walkways.

17.8.5.6 The inspector should inspect for chimney outlets that jeopardize people's safety, overheat combustible structures, or that might cause flue gases to enter nearby building openings.

17.8.5.7 The inspector should inspect the crowns of masonry chimneys for slopes that direct water into flues.

17.8.6 Flues and Liners

17.8.6.1 The inspector should inspect for galvanized flues and connectors. Flues and connectors should not be galvanized.

17.8.6.2 The inspector should inspect readily accessible and visible flues for rust or corrosion.

17.8.6.3 The inspector should inspect for masonry chimneys that are not lined. All masonry chimneys should be lined.

17.8.6.4 The inspector should inspect for linings that don't extend the entire length of the chimney to a level of 2 inches or more above the crown, splay or wash.

17.8.6.5 The inspector should inspect for liners that are visibly softened, cracked, deteriorated or damaged.

17.8.6.6 The inspector should inspect readily accessible and visible flues and liners for excessive accumulation of creosote, soot, or other combustible material.

17.8.6.7 The inspector should inspect for flues that have two or more openings at the same level.

17.8.6.8 The inspector should inspect for venting into the space around and between liners. The remaining space surrounding a chimney liner should not be used as a vent.

17.8.7 Flue Size

The inspector should inspect the size of the flue, if visible, and compare it to the size of the fireplace opening. This relationship is the most important factor in achieving sufficient draft. A flue that is too small relative to the fireplace opening will be unable to lift and remove hazardous flue gases to the outside.

17.8.8 Connectors (Solid Wood-Burning Appliance to Chimney)

17.8.8.1 The inspector should inspect for connectors from solid fuel-burning appliances that have a rise to the chimney of less than ¼-inch per foot.

17.8.8.2 The inspector should inspect for connectors that are not as short or straight as practicable.

17.8.8.3 The inspector should inspect for connectors that are covered with insulation.

17.8.8.4 The inspector should inspect for connectors of natural-draft appliances connected to the positive-pressure side of a mechanical draft system.

17.8.8.5 The inspector should inspect for larger connectors entering a flue above smaller connectors.

17.8.9 Cleanouts

17.8.9.1 The inspector should inspect cleanouts for doors and frames that are not made of metal, pre-cast cement, or other non-combustible material.

17.8.9.2 The inspector should inspect combustible materials projecting beyond the faces of chimneys that are within 18 inches of cleanout openings.

17.8.9.3 The inspector should inspect for combustible materials stored within 18 inches of cleanout doors.

17.8.9.4 The inspector should inspect cleanout doors that are obstructed or do not close tightly.

17.8.9.5 The inspector should inspect the interior cleanout's lower edge for heights above the lowest accessible floor level that are less than 16 inches.

17.8.9.6 The inspector should inspect the exterior cleanout's lower edge for heights above grade that are less than 16 inches.

17.8.9.7 The inspector should inspect the bases of chimney flues for distances that are not between 6 and 12 inches below the bottom edges of their cleanout openings.

Sample Reporting Language

Fireplace and Chimney Inspection Report

Client: _____

Location of fireplace and chimney: _____

This inspection was performed in substantial compliance with the International Standards of Practice for Performing a General Home Inspection. The inspection shall include examination of readily accessible and visible portions of solid fuel-burning, low-heat fireplaces and chimneys. The inspection is not all-inclusive or technically exhaustive. The goal of this inspection is to provide observations that may lead to the decrease of the hazards associated with fireplaces and chimneys.

___The inspector noted solid fuel-burning appliances or fireplaces located where gasoline or other flammable vapors or gases were present.

___The inspector noted unused openings in chimneys or flues.

___The inspector noted missing smoke detectors. A smoke detector should be installed in the same room as the fireplace.

International Phase I Standards of Practice for Inspecting Fireplaces and Chimneys

___The inspector noted missing carbon-monoxide detectors. A carbon-monoxide detector should be installed in the same room as the fireplace.

___The inspector noted a combustible lintel over the fireplace opening.

___The inspector noted combustible material within 6 inches above the fireplace opening that projected out less than 1½ inches from the face of the fireplace.

___The inspector noted combustible material within 12 inches above the fireplace opening that projected out more than 1½ inches from the face of the fireplace.

___The inspector noted the throat or damper was located less than 8 inches above the fireplace opening.

___The inspector noted that the manually operated damper did not operate or close properly.

___The inspector noted that the damper or damper components had rust or corrosion.

___The inspector noted that the hearth extension had a thickness of less than 2 inches.

___The inspector noted that the hearth extension was less than 16 inches in front of or less than 8 inches beyond each side of the opening (for a fireplace opening less than 6 square feet).

___The inspector noted that the hearth extension was less than 20 inches in front of or less than 12 inches beyond each side of the opening (for a fireplace opening 6 square feet or greater).

___The inspector noted hearths, hearth extensions or chambers that had joint separation, damage or deterioration.

___The inspector noted single-wall metal chimneys in a one- or two-family dwelling. Single-wall metal chimneys should not be used in one- and two-family dwellings.

___The inspector noted wall protectors (heat shields) with less than 1-inch air gaps.

___The inspector noted an exposed interior single-wall metal chimney that was not continuously enclosed where it extended through closets, storage areas, or habitable spaces, or where the surface of the chimney could come into contact with combustible materials or people.

___The inspector noted an interior single-wall metal chimney that was less than 18 inches away from a wood-framed wall or combustible material.

___The inspector noted an interior single-wall metal chimney 18 inches or under in diameter that was less than 2 inches away from a non-combustible wall.

___The inspector noted an interior single-wall metal chimney over 18 inches in diameter that was less than 4 inches away from a non-combustible wall.

___The inspector noted that the distance between an exterior-mounted, single-wall metal chimney was less than 2 feet away from a door, window or walkway.

___The inspector noted that the distance between an exterior-mounted, single-wall metal chimney was less than 18 inches away from a wood-framed wall or combustible material.

___The inspector noted that the distance between an exterior-mounted, single-wall metal chimney 18 inches or under in diameter was less than 2 inches away from a non-combustible wall.

___The inspector noted that the distance between an exterior-mounted, single-wall metal chimney over 18 inches in diameter was less than 4 inches away from a non-combustible wall.

_X_ The inspector noted a missing thimble where a chimney passed through a combustible roof.

_X_ The inspector noted a chimney that terminated less than 3 feet above the highest point where it passed through a roof surface.

_X_ The inspector noted a chimney that terminated less than 2 feet above a portion of a building (ridge, wall or parapet) within 10 feet.

___The inspector noted a chimney that terminated less than 3 feet from an adjacent building or building opening.

_X_ The inspector noted a chimney that terminated less than 10 feet above grade or a walkway.

___The inspector noted a chimney outlet that jeopardized people's safety, overheated combustible structures, or that might cause flue gases to enter nearby building openings.

_X_ The inspector noted the slope of a crown of a masonry chimney that directed water into the flue.

___The inspector noted galvanized flues or connectors. Flues and connectors should not be galvanized.

_X_ The inspector noted a rusted or corroded flue.

_X_ The inspector noted a masonry chimney that was not lined. All masonry chimneys should be lined.

_X_ The inspector noted a lining that didn't extend the entire length of the chimney to a level of 4 inches or more above the crown, splay or wash.

___The inspector noted a liner that was visibly softened, cracked, deteriorated or damaged.

___The inspector noted a liner that had an excessive accumulation of creosote, soot, or other combustible material.

_X_ The inspector noted a flue that had two or more openings at the same level.

___The inspector noted an appliance venting into the space around and between liners. The remaining space surrounding a chimney liner should not be used as a vent.

___The inspector noted that the size of the flue was too small relative to the size of the fireplace opening. This relationship is the most important factor in achieving sufficient draft. A flue that is too small relative to the fireplace opening will be unable to lift and remove hazardous flue gases to the outside.

_X_ The inspector noted a connector from a solid fuel-burning appliance that had a rise to the chimney of less than 1/4-inch per foot.

___The inspector noted a connector that was not as short or straight as practicable.

International Phase I Standards of Practice for Inspecting Fireplaces and Chimneys

___The inspector noted a connector that was covered with insulation.

___The inspector noted a connector of a natural-draft appliance connected to the positive-pressure side of a mechanical draft system.

___The inspector noted a larger connector entering the flue above a smaller connector.

___The inspector noted a cleanout door or frame that was not made of metal, pre-cast cement, or other non-combustible material.

___The inspector noted combustible materials projecting beyond the face of the chimney that were within 18 inches of a cleanout opening.

___The inspector noted combustible materials stored within 18 inches of a cleanout door.

___The inspector noted a cleanout door that was obstructed or did not close tightly.

___The inspector noted that the height of an interior cleanout's lower edge was less than 16 inches above the lowest accessible floor level.

___The inspector noted that the height of an exterior cleanout's lower edge was less than 16 inches above grade.

___The inspector noted that the base of a chimney flue was not between 6 and 12 inches below the bottom edge of its cleanout opening.

This inspection was performed by: _____

Signature: _____

Date: _____

Quiz #10

1. T/F: Chimneys are structurally invulnerable.

    ☐ True
    ☐ False

2. T/F: Efflorescence is a cosmetic issue only.

    ☐ True
    ☐ False

3. When _____ leads to strong osmotic pressures—greater than the strength of the building material—and the material literally breaks apart, the resulting damage is called _____.

    ☐ efflorescence, spalling
    ☐ spalling, efflorescence

4. _____ can create pressure that is greater than the structural strength of concrete, which can be from 2,000 psi to 3,000 psi.

    ☐ Osmosis
    ☐ Water vapor diffusion
    ☐ Water intrusion
    ☐ Capillary action

5. Porous building materials are capable of wicking water for large distances due to _____ action.

    ☐ capillary
    ☐ osmotic
    ☐ seismic

6. Building materials, such as concrete, wood, brick and stone, are _____ materials.

    ☐ porous
    ☐ impermeable
    ☐ semi-permeable

7. _____ is the dissolved salts deposited on the surface of a material (such as concrete or brick) that are visible after the evaporation of the water that transported them.

    ☐ Spalling
    ☐ Efflorescence
    ☐ Osmosis

8. _____ is a common repair for deteriorated mortar joints.

☐ Repointing
☐ Firebricking
☐ Cricketing

9. T/F: Kickout flashing should not be installed when stucco or EIFS is installed.

☐ True
☐ False

10. The main purpose of the kickout flashing is to divert water away from the exterior roof-covering materials and into the _____.

☐ gutter
☐ fireplace
☐ main vent stack

11. A missing kickout flashing often results in concentrated areas of _____ accumulation and potentially severe damage to exterior walls.

☐ electrical conductivity
☐ snow
☐ water

12. Water penetration into the cladding can occasionally be observed on the exterior wall in the form of _____ water stains.

☐ diagonal
☐ horizontal
☐ vertical

Answer Key is on page 76.

Safe Practices for Fireplaces

The fireplace damper must be fully open before starting a fire, and left open until the fire is completely out.

Fireplaces should not be overloaded with firewood.

Green or wet wood should never be used.

Screens should be closed during the fireplace's operation to prevent sparks from flying out into the room.

Glass door enclosures can be closed to reduce heat loss from the room into the chimney.

Glass doors on a factory-built fireplace must be tested and listed for that particular fireplace. It can be dangerous to use the wrong set of glass doors.

A wood stove (freestanding or insert style) should never be installed in a factory-built fireplace system unless the insert has been tested and listed for such use.

Annual chimney inspections and sweeping are recommended.

Fireplace Safety for Homeowners

More than one-third of Americans use fireplaces, wood stoves, and other fuel-fired appliances as primary heat sources in their homes. Unfortunately, many people are unaware of the fire risks when heating with wood and solid fuels.

Heating fires account for 36% of residential home fires in rural areas every year. These fires are often due to creosote buildup in chimneys and stovepipes. All home heating systems require regular maintenance to function safely and efficiently.

InterNACHI® encourages homeowners to practice the following fire safety steps to keep those home fires safely burning. Remember, fire safety is a personal responsibility.

Keep Fireplaces and Wood Stoves Clean

Have your chimney or wood stove inspected and cleaned annually by a certified chimney specialist.

Keep the area around the hearth clear of debris, decorations, and flammable materials.

Leave glass doors open while burning a fire. Leaving the doors open ensures that the fire receives enough air to complete combustion, and it keeps creosote from building up in the chimney.

Close glass doors when the fire is out to prevent air from the chimney opening from getting into the room. Most glass fireplace doors have a metal mesh screen, which should be closed when the glass doors are open. This mesh screen helps keep embers from getting out of the fireplace area.

Safe Practices for Fireplaces

Always use a metal mesh screen with fireplaces that do not have a glass fireplace door.

Install a stovepipe thermometer to help monitor the flue temperature.

Keep air inlets on wood stoves open, and never restrict the air supply to a fireplace. Otherwise, creosote may build up, which could lead to a chimney fire.

Use fire-resistant materials on the walls around a wood stove.

Safely Burn Fuels

Never use flammable liquids to start a fire.

Use only seasoned hardwood. Soft, damp wood accelerates creosote buildup. In pellet stoves, burn only dry, seasoned wood pellets.

Build small fires that burn completely and produce less smoke.

Never burn cardboard boxes, trash, or other debris in your fireplace or wood stove.

When building a fire, place logs at the rear of the fireplace on an adequate supporting grate.

Never leave a fire in the fireplace unattended. Extinguish the fire before going to bed or leaving the house.

Allow ashes to cool before disposing of them. Place ashes in a tightly covered metal container, and keep the ash container at least 10 feet away from your home and any other nearby buildings. Never empty the ash directly into a trashcan. Douse and saturate the ashes with water.

Protect the Outside of Your Home

Stack firewood outdoors at least 30 feet away from your home.

Keep the roof clear of leaves, pine needles, and other debris.

Cover the chimney with a mesh screen spark arrester.

Extend all vent pipes at least three feet above the roof.

Remove branches hanging above the chimney, flues and vents.

Protect the Inside of Your Home

Install smoke alarms on every level of your home, and inside and outside of each sleeping area. Test them monthly, and change the batteries at least once a year. Consider installing the new long-life smoke alarms.

Provide proper venting systems for all heating equipment.

Fire Extinguishers

A fire extinguisher is used to douse fire and prevent its spread. It's a small metal canister that contains compressed gas (usually nitrogen) that, when activated, propels a directed spray of flame-retardant chemicals. Fire extinguishers are only effective if building occupants understand where and why they are used.

Fire Type

Fire extinguishers are distinguished based on the types of fires against which they're effective. These fires are classified by their fuel source, and assigned identifying letters as follows:

- A Class: This extinguisher is used against fires that result from ordinary combustibles, such as wood and paper.

- B Class: This extinguisher is used against fires that result from combustible liquids, such as kerosene, gasoline, oil and grease.

- C Class: This extinguisher is used against fires of an electrical nature. These result from the combustion of circuit breakers, wires, outlets, and other electrical devices and equipment. Extinguishers designed to handle this type of fire cannot use chemicals that are conductive, since conductive agents increase the risk of electric shock to the operator.

- D Class: This extinguisher is used against fires that result from combustible metals, such as sodium, potassium, titanium, and magnesium. These fires occur mostly in chemical laboratories and are rare in most other environments.

- K Class: This extinguisher is used against fires that consume vegetable oils and animal fats, and are used for fires that generally happen in kitchens.

NOTE: Although the letter rankings listed above refer to fire types, these symbols can also be used to identify the extinguishers themselves. For instance, an extinguisher that uses CO_2 can be called a CO_2 extinguisher or a BC extinguisher.

Extinguisher Types

No fire extinguisher can be safely or effectively used for every type of fire. Some contain chemicals that are ineffective in certain situations, and can even cause harm to the operator if misapplied. To prevent confusion, extinguishers are classified by the type of chemical agents they contain. A few of the most common extinguisher types are listed below.

- Dry Chemical: There are two types of fire extinguishers that use a dry chemical.

    One is called multi-purpose dry chemical and uses ammonium phosphate as the extinguishing agent, which is effective on A, B and C Class fires. This chemical is corrosive and must be scrubbed from surfaces after use. These types of extinguishers are very common and are found in schools, homes, hospitals and offices.

    Sodium bicarbonate is used in extinguishers known as regular dry chemical, which are capable of handling B and C Class fires. These extinguishers are found in garages, kitchens and laboratories. Sodium bicarbonate is easy to clean and non-toxic.

- Carbon Dioxide: These extinguishers contain liquid CO_2 that is expelled as a gas. They are effective against B and C Class fires. Unlike other chemicals, CO_2 does not leave a harmful residue and is environmentally friendly. It also poses very little danger to electronics, and is effectively employed in laboratories, computer rooms, and other areas with sensitive equipment.
- Water Extinguishers: These extinguishers are most suited for A Class fires. However, they cannot be used in B, C or D Class fires. In B and D Class fires, the water will spread the flames. In a C Class fire, the water is conductive and poses a risk of electric shock to the operator. However, the misting nozzle of a water mist extinguisher breaks up the stream of de-ionized water so that there is no conductive path back to the operator. Since the agent used is water, these types of extinguishers are inexpensive and environmentally friendly.
- Wet Chemical Fire Extinguishers: These devices are designed to combat K Class fires and commonly use potassium acetate. They are appropriately employed in commercial kitchens and restaurants, especially around deep fryers. The chemical is emitted as a fine mist that does not cause grease to splash onto other surfaces. They can also be used in A Class fires.

Inspection of Extinguishers

InterNACHI® inspectors should:

- check that a portable fire extinguisher exists within a 30-foot travel distance of commercial-type cooking equipment that uses cooking oil or animal fat;
- check that a portable fire extinguisher is within 75 feet of travel on every floor;
- check for the presence of portable extinguishers, and determine that they are located in conspicuous and readily available locations immediately available for use, and not obscured from view;
- confirm that access to extinguishers is not obstructed;
- make sure that the hose (if so equipped) is intact and not obstructed;
- make sure the pressure dial reads in the green or "charged" area. It should also be clear and readable;
- check that the pull pin is securely fastened within the handle and held in place by the anti-tamper seal;
- check for visible dents or cracks in the extinguisher's canister;
- check that the extinguisher is in its proper location and mounted correctly;
- check for modifications that might reduce the extinguisher's functionality; and
- make sure that the fire extinguisher has a label and that it is legible.

Inspectors should not do the following:

- test fire extinguishers.
- determine the adequate number of fire extinguishers needed or their ratings.
- ignite or extinguish fires.

Extinguisher Testing and Replacement

The National Fire Protection Agency (NFPA) recommends that extinguishers be tested every five or 12 years, depending on the type. The standard method of testing (hydrostatic) is conducted underwater where the cylinders are subjected to pressures that exceed their ratings. Vessels that fail the test are condemned and destroyed, while the rest are reassembled and put back into service.

According to the NFPA, extinguishers should not be tested but destroyed instead if any of the following conditions are present:

- evidence of repair by soldering, welding, brazing, or the use of patching compounds.
- the cylinder threads are worn, corroded, broken, cracked or nicked.
- there is corrosion that has caused pitting, including pitting under a removable nameplate or nameband assembly.
- the fire extinguisher has been burned in a fire.
- a calcium chloride-type of extinguisher agent was used in a stainless steel fire extinguisher.
- the shell is of copper or brass construction joined by soft solder or rivets.
- the depth of a dent exceeds one-tenth of the greatest dimension of the dent if not in a weld, or exceeds 1/4-inch if the dent includes a weld.
- any local or general corrosion, cuts, gouges or dings have removed more than 10% of the minimum cylinder wall thickness.
- a fire extinguisher has been used for any purpose other than to extinguish a fire.

When should a fire extinguisher be used?

Small fires can be controlled through the use of household or commercial fire extinguishers. A household extinguisher can often completely douse a very small fire and prevent the need for professional assistance. Even if a fire cannot be completely doused, a homeowner can potentially control a blaze with an extinguisher long enough for firefighters to arrive. A fire extinguisher should not be used if the operator is not sure if he has the proper type of extinguisher, if he's not sure how to use it, if he cannot avoid smoke, or if he is in imminent danger. If the operation of an extinguisher will place building occupants in danger, they should evacuate the building and wait for fire crews to arrive.

What is on an extinguisher's label? You'll find:

- essential information about the types of fires it can combat. Newer devices have pictures that correspond directly to the fire types listed above. Older models have letters that serve the same purpose;
- a numerical rating that designates the extinguishing potential for that particular model (Class A and B);
- instructions for operation; and
- a tag that indicates if and when an inspection occurred.

Do fire extinguishers expire?

Fire extinguishers expire, and they do this for a few different reasons. One common way is that, over time, the seal on the neck will weaken and allow compressed gas to escape. Extinguishers that have lost much of their pressure will not operate properly. Pressure within an extinguisher can be conveniently checked through a pressure gauge. ABC-Class extinguishers (ammonium phosphate) have the tendency to fail due to solidification of the chemical in the canister base. Homeowners and inspectors can delay this process by periodically shaking the extinguisher. Expensive extinguishers that have expired, especially those designed for commercial use, can be refilled and resealed by companies that specialize in this service. Inexpensive models are disposable.

Unfortunately, an expiration date cannot be fully trusted, and there is no foolproof way to know if an extinguisher is no longer functional. Due to the extremely destructive potential of fires and the relatively low cost of extinguishers, it is advisable to replace or recharge questionable extinguishers.

In summary, extinguishers are classified based on their chemical ingredients, all of which have their own strengths and limitations. It is important to know which type of extinguisher combats what type of fire. Fire extinguishers are critical indoor components that must be maintained and inspected regularly.

Take InterNACHI's free, online "Inspecting Portable Fire Extinguishers" course at
www.nachi.org/portable-fire-extinguishers-course

Fireplace Fuel

Fireplaces and wood stoves are designed to burn only one type of fuel. Used as all-purpose incinerators, these devices can pose the following hazards:

- Harmful vapors can vent into the living space. Even the most efficient fireplaces will vent directly into the living space while they're opened and closed for cleaning and refueling, exposing everyone in the house to potentially dangerous fumes.

- Harmful vapors will vent to the outdoors. Most newer fireplaces and wood stoves do an excellent job of funneling smoke and fumes to the outdoors, but the problem doesn't end there; this pollution persists, contaminating household and environmental air.

- Burning inappropriate fuel can cause mechanical damage. Chimneys can become lined with residue from them, which may lead to a dangerous chimney fire. The fumes from certain items will quickly wear out sensitive components, such as catalytic combustors in wood stoves.

Read the following guidelines to better understand what can and cannot be safely burned in a residential fireplace or wood stove.

What can be burned in a fireplace?

- Dried, cut firewood. An adequate fuel supply consists of a mixture of hardwoods, such as maple and oak, and softwoods, such as fir and pine. Softwoods ignite quickly and are useful in the early stages of the fire, while hardwoods provide a longer-lasting fire, and are best used after preheating the chimney. Despite the different burning characteristics of hardwoods and softwoods, which can be attributed to differences in density, the heat-energy released by burning wood is the same, regardless of species. To dry out wood, it should be stacked in an open area outdoors so that the sun can warm the pieces and the breezes can carry away the moisture.

Poplar, spruce and other softwoods generally dry quickly, as does wood that has been split into small pieces.

Adequately seasoned wood has a moisture content of less than 20%, which can be checked using the following indicators:

- The wood has darkened from a white or cream color to yellow or grey.
- There are cracks or checks in the end grain.
- A hollow sound is produced when two pieces of wood are banged together.
- You can split a piece and feel if the new surface is damp or dry.
- The wood does not hiss while burning.
- You can check its moisture content with a moisture meter.

- Pallets. Generally, pallets are safe to burn in fireplaces, although those that are treated with the fumigant methyl bromide (labeled with the initials MB) are unsafe to burn. Also, pallets may have been exposed to a variety of chemicals while they were in use. Aside from these concerns, pallets produce a hot flame because they're usually very dry and their segments are thin. Be careful to check for nails while cutting pallets, as they may damage a saw blade. You may also wind up with nails in your ash, which should be disposed of far from roads and driveways.
- Fallen tree limbs. These can generally be collected and used for kindling, provided they have been given time to dry.
- Wood collected from housing developments. If it is truly trash and not someone's property (including the housing contractor's), using scavenged wood that has been cleared away for housing developments is good for burning. Try to obtain it before the non-lumber grade wood is pushed into massive piles and burned as a means of disposal by the contractor.
- Fire logs. These artificial logs burn relatively cleanly and release less ash than their natural wood counterparts.

What should never be burned in a fireplace?

- Painted wood. Paint contains heavy metals, such as lead, chromium and titanium, which are used to make the different colors. These metals, especially lead, can be toxic even in small quantities if inhaled. If you're unsure if your paint has lead, be sure to consult with your InterNACHI® inspector during your next scheduled inspection.
- Pressure-treated wood. Wood is commonly made resistant to fungus and insects through the addition of copper, chromate and arsenic, in a process known as CCA treatment. CCA treatment places roughly 27 grams of arsenic in every 12-foot 2x6, which is sufficient to kill about 250 adults, which is why it is illegal in the U.S. to burn pressure-treated wood. Vaporized CCA wood, known as fly ash, is extremely toxic; in one case, as reported by the American Medical Association, a family was stricken with seizures, hair loss, debilitating headaches, blackouts and nosebleeds from fly ash released when they unknowingly used CCA wood to burn in their fireplace. Even the family's houseplants and fish succumbed to the toxic fumes.
- Plywood, particleboard, chipboard or OSB. When burned, these manmade woods release formaldehyde, and possibly also hydrochloric acid or dioxin. Some states have outlawed the incineration of some or all of these artificial wood products.
- Rotted, diseased or moldy wood. This wood will not burn as long as other wood, may produce bad smells when burned, and could bring insects into the house.

- Damp wood. Wood that has a moisture content higher than 20% will burn inefficiently and will contribute to a greater accumulation of creosote in the chimney, as well as air pollution.

- Allergenic plants. Urushiol, which is the chemical that induces the typically minor allergic reaction when skin is exposed to poison ivy, poison sumac or poison oak, is far more dangerous when inhaled. Urushiol is not destroyed by fire and can quickly cause life-threatening respiratory distress if any of these plants are burned.

- Dryer lint. While it's often used effectively as a fire-starter, lint can contain a wide array of dangerous chemicals that come from your clothes and fabric softener.

- Trash. Never burn household garbage, as it contains a range of potentially hazardous materials and chemicals that react in unpredictable ways when burned together. Newspaper ink, plastics, aluminum foil, plastic baggies, and whatever else constitutes your particular trash can create a deadly chemical cocktail.

- Driftwood. Wood found on the beach of an ocean or salty lake will release salt when burned, which will quickly corrode any metal and etch the glass of a wood stove or fireplace. Catalytic converters are especially vulnerable to salt corrosion. In addition to potential damage to the stove or fireplace, the EPA claims that driftwood releases toxic chemicals when burned.

In summary, use only approved and appropriate fuel to burn in your fireplace or wood stove because certain items should never be burned, as they can cause problems ranging from minor irritation to a hazardous health threat to your family.

Quiz #11

1. T/F: It's okay to burn pressure-treated wood.
   - ☐ True
   - ☐ False

2. T/F: It's okay to burn pallets.
   - ☐ True
   - ☐ False

3. T/F: The National Fire Protection Agency (NFPA) recommends that extinguishers be tested every five or 12 years, depending on the type.
   - ☐ True
   - ☐ False

4. T/F: No fire extinguisher can be safely or effectively used for every type of fire.
   - ☐ True
   - ☐ False

5. Fires that result from ordinary combustibles, such as wood and paper, are Class _____.
   - ☐ B
   - ☐ C
   - ☐ A

6. Fires that result from combustible liquids, such as kerosene, gasoline, oil and grease, are Class _____.
   - ☐ B
   - ☐ C
   - ☐ A

7. Fires of an electrical nature are Class _____.
   - ☐ A
   - ☐ C
   - ☐ B

8. Fires resulting from combustible metals, such as sodium, potassium, titanium, and magnesium, are Class _____.
   - ☐ A
   - ☐ B
   - ☐ D

Answer Key is on page 77.

Ventless / Unvented Combustion Appliances

It is recommended that unvented combustion appliances not be installed within the conditioned space of the home. Unvented combustion appliances include unvented fireplaces, also known as ventless, vent-free, or ductless fireplaces. These gas, propane, or ethanol-burning fireplaces have no vent, so they draw combustion air from the room they are in and release toxic combustion byproducts and moisture vapor back into the space in which they are located. Their use is banned in many states and municipalities.

For aesthetic reasons, builders will sometimes install a ventless gas, propane, or ethanol-burning fireplace in the home. These ventless appliances have real flames, providing the ambiance of a traditional fireplace, with convenience and cost savings for the builder because no chimney needs to be installed.

Manufacturers report that they burn at nearly 100% efficiency, releasing fewer harmful gases into the home than other types of fireplaces. However, because they are ventless, any unburned combustion byproducts are released directly into the living space because there is no chimney to vent them out of the home. Also, because no air intake is installed, many manufacturers recommend that homeowners open a window during operation of the fireplace, although there is no way to guarantee that homeowners will follow this advice.

A ventless fireplace that is burning efficiently will have a primarily blue flame. Defects such as plugged burner ports, a cracked burner, excessive gas input, impurities in the gas, or a gas leak somewhere in the unit can impact performance, reducing the efficiency of the burn and increasing the amount of combustion byproducts released.

In addition to possible combustion byproducts, ventless combustion appliances also release significant amounts of water vapor into the air. These products produce 1 gallon of water vapor for every 100,000 BTUs, so a 30,000-BTU appliance would release nearly 1 gallon of water vapor for every three hours of operation, adding significantly to indoor humidity levels.

Due to safety, health, and moisture concerns, some building scientists recommend that unvented appliances not be installed in homes. ENERGY STAR Version 3.0 permits their installation but requires that an inspector test the appliance using a portable CO monitoring device and verify that the ambient CO level does not exceed 35 parts per million (ppm). The inspector should also confirm that the room size provides a minimum volume of combustion air for safe operation of the size of the appliance installed, as specified by the manufacturer and/or building code. The National Fuel Gas Code prohibits the installation of ventless combustion heaters in bathrooms and bedrooms.

Some ventless fireplaces come equipped by the manufacturer with an oxygen-detection sensor that will automatically shut down the appliance if oxygen levels in the room become too low. InterNACHI® recommends that the homeowner install a CO detector in the room near the ventless fireplace, in the same room.

Because of safety concerns, several states and municipalities have banned the use of ventless combustion appliances.

How to check unvented combustion appliances:

- Turn on or light the ventless combustion fireplace.
- Let the appliance operate for 10 minutes.

- Use a portable, hand-held CO monitor in the air within a few feet of the fireplace or appliance to test the ambient air near it. If the CO level is above 35 ppm, the appliance fails the test and must be serviced and re-tested, or replaced.

Can the health hazards of an unvented heater be reduced?

The most effective method to reduce the hazards is to discontinue use of the unvented combustion appliance by switching to a vented gas or electric appliance.

Where the use of an unvented gas appliance is permitted, the following safety tips are recommended:

1. Use only approved gas heaters with ODS pilots.
2. Follow all operation and maintenance instructions carefully.
3. Clean the burner yearly, or more often, as required in the owner's manual.
4. Do not use an oversized heater. The Gas Appliance Manufacturers Association recommends limiting the amount of pollutants by correctly sizing the appliance.
5. Do not operate for more than four hours at a time.
6. Do not use unvented fuel-fired heaters in bedrooms, bathrooms, or confined spaces.
7. Provide adequate ventilation, as required in the owner's manual. An outside air source will likely be required.
8. Discontinue the use of unvented combustion appliance if the pollutants cause health problems.
9. Install a UL- or IAS-listed carbon monoxide detector. Because low concentrations of carbon monoxide can cause health problems, the homeowner should install a detector advertised as a "sensitive" detector, or one with a digital display.

Ventilated Fireplaces

Ventilated fireplaces typically burn natural gas or propane and use a vent to bring outside combustion air directly into the firebox to support the fire. These fireplaces have tight-fitting glass doors across their face to prevent conditioned room air from being used as combustion air, and then being expelled through the exhaust. Consuming room air for combustion may deplete oxygen levels in the home. Heat still radiates into the room. Exhaust gases can be expelled vertically up a chimney, or horizontally out a side wall. In addition to saving space and materials, taking away the need for a traditional chimney provides tremendous flexibility in where these fireplaces can be located. These closed combustion systems are much less likely to experience backdrafting, the hazardous situation in which exhaust gases are drawn into the home instead of being expelled to the outdoors, or contribute to backdrafting in other combustion appliances, such as water heaters or furnaces.

Summary

Unvented combustion appliances should not be installed within the conditioned space of the home. Their use is banned in many states and municipalities. Ventilated fireplaces help ensure that dangerous byproducts from burning fossil fuel cannot back-draft into the home.

Quiz #12

1. _____ fireplaces, more accurately known as duct-free fireplaces and room-venting fireplaces, are a type of residential gas-heating device.

    ☐ Masonry
    ☐ Ventless
    ☐ Pre-fabricated

2. T/F: Ventless fireplaces vent unburned combustion byproducts directly into the living space.

    ☐ True
    ☐ False

3. T/F: Several states in the U.S., as well as Canada and other countries, have outlawed ventless gas fireplaces due to safety concerns.

    ☐ True
    ☐ False

4. If the ventless fireplace is oversized for the square footage of the area to be heated, then that condition is considered _____.

    ☐ safe
    ☐ a defect

Answer Key is on page 77.

Appendix I: Answer Keys

Answer Key for Quiz #1

1. T/F: The inspector is required to inspect the damper doors by opening and closing them, if readily accessible and manually operable.
Answer: **True**

2. The inspection is **a visual-only evaluation of the accessible** chimney and fireplace structure, systems and components.

3. T/F: The inspector should look at the general structure of the chimney and any connections to appliances, stoves, and heating systems.
Answer: **True**

4. T/F: The inspector should advise his/her client that all fireplaces, fuel-burning stoves, and chimneys should be inspected by a certified chimney sweep prior to their first use, and not less than annually.
Answer: **True**

Answer Key for Quiz #2

1. Footings for masonry chimneys must be made of concrete or solid masonry at least **1 foot** thick.

2. The footing for a masonry chimney should extend at least **6** inches beyond the face of the fireplace or foundation wall on all sides.

3. Footings for masonry fireplaces must extend **below** the frost line.

4. House framing components should be at least **2** inches away from the chimney wall.

5. Open spaces between the chimney wall and the combustible building materials should be sealed and insulated with **non-combustible** material.

6. A masonry chimney should extend at least **3** feet above the highest point where the chimney passes through the roof, and **2** feet above any portion of a building that is within a **10**-foot distance horizontally.

7. Inlets to masonry chimneys must enter from the **side**.

Answer Key for Quiz #3

1. T/F: Gas vents that are greater than 12 inches in size or that are located less than 8 feet from a vertical wall or similar structure should terminate at least 2 feet above the highest point where they pass through the roof, and not less than 2 feet above any portion of a dwelling within 10 feet horizontally.
Answer: **True**

2. T/F: A greater height for a fuel-gas vent above the roof is needed as the roof pitch approaches being a vertical surface.
Answer: **True**

Appendix I: Answer Keys

3. T/F: It is a common mistake to apply height requirements for chimney terminations (such as the 3-2-10 Rule) to fuel vents that cause them to extend above roofs much higher than needed, in most cases.
Answer: **True**

4. T/F: The venting system is permitted to extend into or pass through a fabricated air duct or furnace plenum.
Answer: **False**

5. T/F: A cast-in-place chimney flue liner is made of a lightweight, cement-like product installed inside the chimney.
Answer: **True**

6. A cast-in-place lining **can** help correct the structural integrity of an old chimney.

7. Metal chimney flue liners are usually made of **stainless steel** or aluminum.

8. T/F: Stainless steel flue lining is suitable for wood-burning, gas, or oil applications.
Answer: **True**

9. Clay tiles are the **most** common type of masonry chimney liner.

10. The general rule is that a single flue should be used for only **one** heating system(s).

Answer Key for Quiz #4

1. T/F: Chimneys should extend at least 2 feet higher than any portion of a building within 10 feet, but shall not be less than 3 feet above the highest point where the chimney passes through the roof.
Answer: **True**

2. Type L venting systems should terminate with a listed and labeled cap at least **2** feet above the roof and at least **2** feet above any portion of the building within **10** feet.

3. T/F: It may be difficult to tell the difference between Type L and Type B vents because they are made from similar components.
Answer: **True**

4. Type **L** vents are designed for venting approved oil-fired and natural-gas appliances.

5. T/F: Type L vents must not be used to vent coal- or wood-fired appliances.
Answer: **True**

6. Type **B** vents must be equipped with their own special chimney caps.

7. Type **B** vents are vents suitable only for listed, draft hood-equipped, gas-fired appliances, including most domestic heating and hot water systems.

Answer Key for Quiz #5

1. **All** masonry chimneys should have a concrete, metal or stone cap.

2. The flue liner tile should project above the masonry cap **a minimum of 4 inches**.

3. A proper masonry chimney cap should be constructed of a Portland cement-based mixture and cast or formed so it provides an overhang projecting beyond all sides of the chimney by a minimum of **2** inches.

4. Most masonry chimneys are built with an inadequate cap constructed from common **mortar mix**.

5. The chimney **crown** is the top element of a masonry chimney.

6. If the chimney has a dimension parallel to the ridgeline greater than 30 inches, and does not intersect the ridgeline, a chimney **cricket** must be provided.

7. T/F: Chimney flashing should be installed where the chimney stack meets the roof covering to prevent water penetration.
   Answer: **True**

Answer Key for Quiz #6

1. The smoke shelf is located behind the **damper**.

2. T/F: One purpose of the opened damper door is to prevent the downdraft from pushing smoke into the room.
   Answer: **True**

3. The damper must be operable from **the room containing the fireplace**.

4. T/F: The throat of the fireplace is located below the combustion chamber.
   Answer: **False**

5. T/F: The throat of the fireplace controls the efficiency of the fireplace.
   Answer: **True**

6. T/F: The fireplace firebox walls are slanted to reflect heat energy into the room.
   Answer: **True**

7. T/F: The space inside the fireplace is called the firebox.
   Answer: **True**

8. T/F: The size of the fireplace is based on the size of the room.
   Answer: **True**

9. The **lintel** is located over the fireplace opening and supports the masonry above.

10. Fireplace hearths are typically made of **concrete or masonry**.

11. T/F: The back hearth is made up of compacted earth that can withstand heat from fire.
    Answer: **False**

Appendix I: Answer Keys

Answer Key for Quiz #7

1. If the factory-built fireplace is located on an exterior wall, a **chase** can be constructed around the chimney to contain and protect it.

2. T/F: Chimneys for factory-built fireplaces require specific clearances and support components.
Answer: **True**

3. T/F: The openings through which the chimneys of factory-built fireplaces pass should be blocked with fire-stop spacers and support boxes.
Answer: **True**

4. T/F: Factory-built chimneys are not required to be of masonry construction.
Answer: **True**

5. The top of a factory-built chimney has a **storm collar** to divert rainwater from the chimney pipe to the chimney flashing.

6. A factory-built fireplace is **less** expensive to install than a masonry fireplace.

7. T/F: A factory-built fireplace has a zero clearance requirement to combustibles.
Answer: **True**

Answer Key for Quiz #8

1. Wood that has a moisture content of less than **20**% burns hotter and cleaner than freshly cut wood.

2. In **catalytic** stoves, the smoky exhaust passes through a coated, ceramic honeycomb that ignites particulates and smoke gases.

3. **Non-catalytic** stoves have three characteristics that assist in complete, clean combustion: pre-heated combustion air introduced from above the fuel; firebox insulation; and a large baffle.

4. **Smoke** from wood stoves can cause a variety of health ailments, from asthma to cancer.

5. T/F: It is safe to burn coal in a wood stove.
Answer: **False**

6. T/F: It is safe to dispose of ashes from a wood stove using a central vacuum system.
Answer: **False**

7. T/F: Homeowners should periodically remove the stovepipe between the stove and the chimney so that it can be inspected for creosote.
Answer: **True**

Answer Key for Quiz #9

1. T/F: The inspector should inspect cleanouts for doors and frames that are not made of ferrous metal, pre-cast cement, or other non-combustible material.
Answer: **True**

2. T/F: The inspector should inspect for connectors from solid fuel-burning appliances that have a rise to the chimney of less than 1/4-inch per foot.
Answer: **True**

3. T/F: Flue and connector pipes should be galvanized.
Answer: **False**

4. T/F: The inspector should inspect for flues that have two or more openings at the same level.
Answer: **True**

5. The inspector should inspect for chimneys that terminate less than **3** feet above the highest point where they pass through the roof surface.

6. T/F: Single-wall metal chimneys should always be used in one- and two-family dwellings.
Answer: **False**

7. T/F: The inspector should inspect for hearths that are not made of concrete or masonry.
Answer: **True**

8. T/F: The inspector should inspect for combustible lintels above fireplace openings.
Answer: **True**

Answer Key for Quiz #10

1. T/F: Chimneys are structurally invulnerable.
Answer: **False**

2. T/F: Efflorescence is a cosmetic issue only.
Answer: **False**

3. When **efflorescence** leads to strong osmotic pressures—greater than the strength of the building material—and the material literally breaks apart, the resulting damage is called **spalling**.

4. **Osmosis** can create pressure that is greater than the structural strength of concrete, which can be from 2,000 psi to 3,000 psi.

5. Porous building materials are capable of wicking water for large distances due to **capillary** action.

6. Building materials, such as concrete, wood, brick and stone, are **porous** materials.

7. **Efflorescence** is the dissolved salts deposited on the surface of a material (such as concrete or brick) that are visible after the evaporation of the water that transported them.

8. **Repointing** is a common repair for deteriorated mortar joints.

9. T/F: Kickout flashing should not be installed when stucco or EIFS is installed.
Answer: **False**

10. The main purpose of the kickout flashing is to divert water away from the exterior roof-covering materials and into the **gutter**.

11. A missing kickout flashing often results in concentrated areas of **water** accumulation and potentially severe damage to exterior walls.

Appendix I: Answer Keys

12. Water penetration into the cladding can occasionally be observed on the exterior wall in the form of **vertical** water stains.

Answer Key for Quiz #11

1. T/F: It's okay to burn pressure-treated wood.
   Answer: **False**

2. T/F: It's okay to burn pallets.
   Answer: **True**

3. T/F: The National Fire Protection Agency (NFPA) recommends that extinguishers be tested every five or 12 years, depending on the type.
   Answer: **True**

4. T/F: No fire extinguisher can be safely or effectively used for every type of fire.
   Answer: **True**

5. Fires that result from ordinary combustibles, such as wood and paper, are Class **A**.

6. Fires that result from combustible liquids, such as kerosene, gasoline, oil and grease, are Class **B**.

7. Fires of an electrical nature are Class **C**.

8. Fires resulting from combustible metals, such as sodium, potassium, titanium, and magnesium, are Class **D**.

Answer Key for Quiz #12

1. **Ventless** fireplaces, more accurately known as duct-free fireplaces and room-venting fireplaces, are a type of residential gas-heating device.

2. T/F: Ventless fireplaces vent unburned combustion byproducts directly into the living space.
   Answer: **True**

3. T/F: Several states in the U.S., as well as Canada and other countries, have outlawed ventless gas fireplaces due to safety concerns.
   Answer: **True**

4. If the ventless fireplace is oversized for the square footage of the area to be heated, then that condition is considered **a defect**.

Notes

EDUCATION & TRAINING BOOKS

Whether you're new to the business, an inspector seeking more information, or a veteran of the industry looking to expand your knowledge, these official InterNACHI® publications will help you become the best inspector you can be.

We Offer the Following Education & Training Books:

- **How to Inspect the Exterior**
  Item Number: 0094

- **How to Perform Deck Inspections**
  Item Number: 0029

- **Residential Plumbing Overview**
  Item Number: 0064

- **Inspecting HVAC Systems**
  Item Number: 0061

- **Safe Practices for the Home Inspector**
  Item Number: 0038

- **Inspecting the Attic, Insulation, Ventilation & Interior**
  Item Number: 0109

- **How to Perform Electrical Inspections**
  Item Number: 0023

- **How to Inspect Pools & Spas**
  Item Number: 0076

- **How to Perform Roof Inspections**
  Item Number: 0042

- **How to Perform a Mold Inspection**
  Item Number: 0022

- **How to Perform Radon Inspections**
  Item Number: 0028

- **Inspecting Foundation Walls and Piers**
  Item Number: 0065

- **25 Standards Every Inspector Should Know**
  Item Number: 0037

- **How to Inspect for Moisture Intrusion**
  Item Number: 0073

- **International Standards of Practice for Inspecting Commercial Properties**
  Item Number: 0016

- **Structural Issues for Home Inspectors**
  Item Number: 0059

The purpose of these publications is to provide accurate and useful information for home inspectors in order to perform an inspection of the various systems at a residential property. They also serve as study aids for InterNACHI's online courses, as well as reference manuals for on the job.

Find these books plus more tools to grow your inspection business at
www.InspectorOutlet.com

INSPECTOR OUTLET

YOU'LL BE SHOCKED BY OUR LOW PRICES!

Inspector Outlet is your source for all things home inspection-related. We are the official store for InterNACHI® publications, equipment and apparel. We strive to provide the best products at the lowest prices in the industry.

InterNACHI® members get the best pricing on tools, testing equipment and meters.

Find an outstanding selection of original training manuals, checklists, articles and PDFs, as well as publications for clients, including the best-selling home maintenance guide, *Now That You've Had a Home Inspection*.

We offer a great line of protective outerwear and customized apparel for home inspectors, including shirts, jackets and hats.

InterNACHI's Inspector Marketing Department can design and print a variety of custom marketing materials for your home inspection business.

Protect yourself and your clients on the job with our specialized safety and inspection equipment that help make your inspections easier and safer.

Are you an InterNACHI® member? Inspector Outlet offers free inspector decals and embroidered patches to all eligible members!

"Inspector Outlet is officially endorsed by InterNACHI for the best prices in the business for our members."
—Nick Gromicko, Founder of InterNACHI®

INSPECTOR OUTLET

www.InspectorOutlet.com   Sales@InspectorOutlet.com